THE
NEW
35MM
PHOTOGRAPHER'S
HANDBOOK

THE
NEW
35MM
PHOTOGRAPHER'S
HANDBOOK

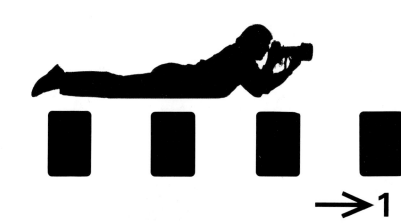

→1

→2

THE
NEW
35MM
PHOTOGRAPHER'S
HANDBOOK

Julian Calder   **John Garrett**

2ND REVISED EDITION

CROWN PUBLISHERS, INC.
NEW YORK

→3

John Garrett was a photographer in his native Australia before settling in England in 1966. He has worked on assignment for most of the world's top magazines including *Time, Paris Match, Stern* and *The Sunday Times*, and has contributed photographs to several books including volumes in the Time-Life series *Cities of the World.*

An experienced photographer who has covered every type of assignment from war to rock concerts and glamour calendars, Garrett is currently engaged on a long-term project— documenting the formative years of his two young sons. Children and travel are Garrett's two main personal interests— both of which are subjects demanding a spontaneous attitude to photography and ideally suited to the 35mm SLR camera.

A Marshall Edition
Conceived, edited and designed by
Marshall Editions Limited
170 Piccadilly London W1V 9DD

Managing Editor: Ruth Binney
Editor: Jinny Johnson

Art Director: John Bigg
Design Editor: Eddie Poulton

Production: Barry Baker
Janice Storr

Library of Congress Cataloging-in-Publication Data
Calder, Julian.
    The new 35 MM photographer's handbook / Julian Calder, John
Garrett. — Rev. ed.
    p.   cm.
    Rev. ed. of: The 35 MM photographer's handbook.   1986.
    ISBN 0-517-57825-5 : $16.95
    1. 35mm cameras.   2. Photography—Handbooks, manuals, etc.
I. Garrett, John.   II. Calder, Julian.   35 MM photographer's
handbook.   III. Title.   IV. Title: New thirty-five MM photographer's
handbook.
TR262.C26   1990
771.3'2—dc20   90-1760
                                                        CIP

Julian Calder's early inspiration came from the great photo stories in *Life Magazine*. He acquired his photographic education at art college and as an assistant to several London photographers. For him, the still photograph has the essential quality of being tangible, involving the viewer in a way that the ephemeral images on television or cinema screen cannot.

He is an inveterate traveller who obtains personal satisfaction from working on assignment for such leading magazines as *Time, Business, The Observer* and *Telegraph* magazines and many other publications. Calder utilizes all the technical gadgetry available in order to realize the full potential of a picture, stretching the versatility of his camera system to the utmost to capture the picture he wants.

First published 1979
© Marshall Editions Ltd
This revised edition first published 1990
© Marshall Editions Developments Ltd
Photographs © 1990 Julian Calder and John Garrett
Text © 1990 Marshall Editions Developments Ltd, Julian Calder and John Garrett
Artwork © 1990 Marshall Editions Developments Ltd

This revised edition first published in the United States in 1990 by Crown Publishers, Inc., 201 East 50th Street, New York, New York 10022

Typeset by Servis Filmsetting Ltd, Manchester, UK

Origination by Gilchrist Bros. Ltd, Leeds, UK, and Reprocolor Llovet SA, Barcelona, Spain

Printed and bound by Usines Brepols SA, Belgium

CONTENTS

Introduction

Since this book was first published I have travelled round the world five times. Assignments have taken me to the North Pole and to the heart of the tropical rain forest and with every trip I have learned more about photography, about ways of getting the pictures I want.

These recent years have seen tremendous advances in all aspects of camera technology. Electronics, printed circuitry, microprocessors, advanced plastics, new film emulsions, flash and zoom lens design—all these developments have conspired to make the world of photography more exciting, more accessible than ever before.

As a professional photographer I have a keen interest in this technology and, in updating *The 35mm Photographer's Handbook* for the nineties, I have looked at what it can do for you—and what it sometimes can't. The text has been completely revised to cover working with the latest equipment and there are more than 150 new pictures whose merit is often enhanced by the technology behind them.

But however many new features a camera has every photographer still needs to know the basics; the camera doesn't take the picture for you. Photography is one of those activities that can only be learned by experience. The more you do it the more you find out and by understanding what went wrong the bad pictures can teach you as much as the good.

This book aims to help you understand fully the creative potential of cameras from the simplest to the most advanced electronic models. It assumes that you wish to take photography seriously; that professional standards of work are what you are after; and that, like a professional, you will want to take pictures every day.

That is why the book has a shape and size to suit the camera bag or a pocket in the car rather than the coffee table. It is meant to be of daily use to architects, teachers and salespeople and to serve myriad other occupations where a picture can speak so much more persuasively than words.

Photography is a world of its own—and a visual access to every other world. It should enhance the recollected pleasures of travel, parenthood and hobbies. Still videos have a long way to go before matching the quality of a Kodachrome transparency or the tonal subtlety of a perfect black and white print.

Most of the pictures in this book were taken on Nikon equipment. Nikon makes one of the most comprehensive 35mm camera systems, but there are another dozen or so systems which are broadly similar. The electronic cameras now available are the most advanced ever. They will be superseded one day but the models featured here will be the basis for camera design for the rest of the century.

Take advantage of all the help technology can offer but don't be daunted or frustrated by it. You the photographer are still in charge. And remember some of the greatest masterpieces of photography have been taken on the simplest cameras.

Julian Calder

SLR cameras

35mm cameras are compact, lightweight and capable of producing a high quality image. Their 36mm × 24mm format is a pleasing shape in which to compose, echoing the age-old golden section theory of design.

SLR stands for single lens reflex. Through this viewing system the photographer sees the exact image that the camera sees. He also benefits from camera metering and can control shutter, aperture and winder without taking his eye from the viewfinder.

The 35mm SLR user has at his disposal the most comprehensive range of interchangeable lenses and accessories, which allow extra versatility and creativity. The small size and weight of modern 35mm systems means that they are fast and easy to use. A fully equipped photographer has both mobility and the capability to operate in any situation.

The new technology

The latest generation of cameras incorporates electronic expertise to make them the most sophisticated yet. Built-in microcomputers control camera functions, process data and evaluate all aspects of your picture.

There are many types of SLR camera on the market, but only a few complete system manufacturers—Nikon, Canon, Olympus, Minolta, Pentax, Contax and Leica. The highly versatile Nikon F-801 illustrated here makes full use of microprocessor circuitry, microelectronics and toughened plastics. It is fully automatic, light and can be used with all Nikon lenses, both autofocus and older models. A camera body used by many professionals as well as amateurs, the F-801 fulfils all the basic requirements of any photographer.

Don't be put off by the sophistication of the new camera technology. It is there to help take good pictures—not just as a gimmick. The new cameras are immensely versatile, but in order to realize the full potential a new owner must, first, read the instruction manual thoroughly

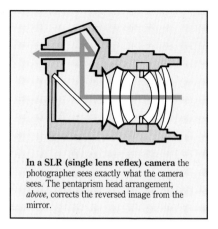

In a SLR (single lens reflex) camera the photographer sees exactly what the camera sees. The pentaprism head arrangement, *above*, corrects the reversed image from the mirror.

and, second, use the camera extensively and analyze the results.

As with any machine, you need to get familiar with a new camera before you see an improvement in pictures. Once used to the camera you will find that features such as autofocus and the various types of automatic metering can solve many photographic problems—sometimes when you didn't even know there was one.

And remember, autofocus and other such features are meant as an aid to, not a substitute for, creative skill. They do not have to be used all the time, only when required—most of the features can be manually controlled. To be in command of the medium a knowledge of the relationship between aperture and shutter is vital, even when working with an electronic camera. But when automatic features are used they free the photographer to concentrate on the picture with the knowledge that other decisions are being taken care of.

Unfortunately, while many cameras make photography more accessible to a wider public, some modern designs appeal more to the jewellery market than to the serious photographer. Cameras are becoming smaller, but since their use is related to the dexterity of the human hand, the limits of miniaturization may have been reached.

Nikon F-801 (N8008)

1 Camera strap eyelet
2 Preview button
3 LCD illumination window
4 Lens mounting index
5 Remote control terminal
6 Focus mode selector
7 Bayonet mount for lens
8 Autofocus lock button
9 Self-timer indicator LED
10 Exposure mode button
11 Metering system selection button
12 Multiple exposure/ film rewind button
13 Accessory shoe
14 Film rewind button
15 Exposure compensation button
16 Shutter release button
17 Power switch
18 Control dial
19 LCD panel
20 Autoexposure lock lever
21 Viewfinder illumination button
22 Viewfinder eyepiece
23 Self-timer button
24 Film cartridge confirmation window
25 Film advance mode button
26 Film speed button

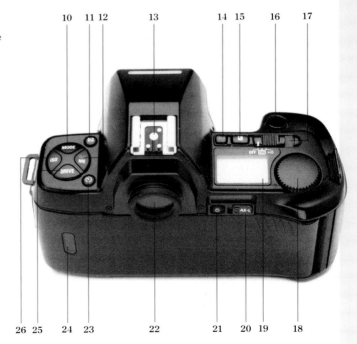

11

Electronic cameras □ 1

Electronics has brought about a revolution in camera technology. The Nikon F-801 (N8008), for example, contains nearly 900 separate parts; these include two powerful microcomputers and eight ICs to process data and help the photographer make the creative decisions necessary to realize a picture.

The use of electronics in such cameras allows them to do more than ever before—it would be impossible to produce mechanical equivalents of all the functions in the F-801. And, despite the complexity of electronic cameras, they are now more reliable than their mechanical counterparts.

1 Meter silicone photo diode (SPD)

2 Microprocessor circuitry (provides lens information to camera circuitry)

3 TTL flash sensor

4 Part semi-silvered mirror (light passes through to the autofocus and spot-metering sensor)

5 Passage of light

6 Autofocus coupling

7 200 CCD (charge couple device) block

8 Charge motor (charges mirror box and shutter unit)

9 Transport motor inside spool

10 Carbon fibre and aluminium shutter blades

11 Shutter block

Electronic cameras □ 2

A central, battery-powered control unit operates all the functions of the electronic camera—shutter, exposure, flash, focusing, information on type of film and number of exposures. Although the camera functions are automatic, the photographer must program in the picture requirements, choosing which mode to shoot in, which metering system to use, and so on. All this information registers on the LED screen, *right*.

The exact terminology used differs according to the camera make, but the following examples explain some of the basic terms in general use:

Mode
Electronic cameras have different operating systems or modes from which the photographer can choose—manual, aperture or shutter priority and three types of programming. Be familiar with the strengths of each system so you can select the one most suitable for each shot.

Programming
Set on programming, the camera selects what it considers to be the correct combination of shutter and aperture for the picture being taken.

High speed programming
The camera automatically selects a fast shutter speed in order to freeze action.

Ordinary programming
The camera selects an aperture that ensures that the picture is sharp from foreground to background.

Shutter priority
You choose the shutter speed for the effect you want. The camera selects the appropriate aperture.

Aperture priority
You choose the aperture for the picture and the camera sets the shutter speed.

Manual
The photographer controls both shutter and aperture—when bracketing, for example.

Autofocus
The lens focuses automatically and shutter won't operate until the subject is sharp.

Metering systems
Electronic cameras have two or three methods of taking the right light reading for the picture.

Matrix or evaluated metering splits the screen into five or six sections and takes an average of them all.

Centre-weighted takes the reading mainly from the centre of the frame where the main interest is likely to be. Spot metering takes the reading from a very small central area.

ISO
This is now the internationally accepted rating system for film speeds, replacing ASA and DIN.

Control dial
This dial is used to select the camera's various functions. Commands are displayed in the viewfinder, *bottom right*, and on the LED screen, *top right*.

LED display
This window on the body of the camera displays all relevant camera information. It is usually displayed for 16 seconds at a time after lightly pressing the shutter button. The illustration, *top right*, shows all possible information on the screen, but this would never appear all at once; the screen, *centre right*, is a representative example.

Balanced fill-in flash
This allows camera and flash unit to be programmed to take a picture in which the flash does not overpower the background light—a complicated procedure before electronic cameras.

Dedicated flash
These flash units work in harmony with, and are controlled by, the camera to take a properly exposed picture. Information is relayed between flash unit and camera via the hot shoe to produce the right amount of flash on the subject.

LED panel

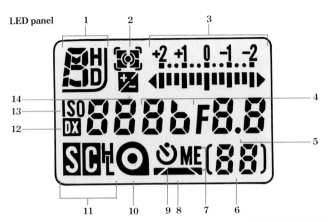

1 Exposure mode
2 Metering system
3 Electronic analog display
4 Shutter/film speeds
5 Aperture/exposure compensation value
6 Frame counter
7 Multiple exposure
8 Film advance and rewind
9 Self-timer
10 Film installation
11 Film advance mode
12 DX-coded film speed setting
13 Film speed setting
14 Exposure compensation

LED panel on Normal Program

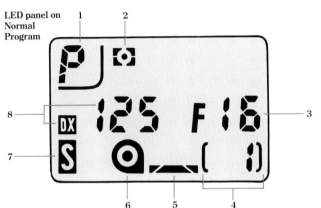

1 Exposure mode: Normal Program
2 Metering system: Matrix
3 Aperture: f16
4 Frame counter: film advanced to first frame
5 Film advance and rewind
6 Film installation: film correctly installed
7 Film advance mode: single frame shooting
8 DX-coded film speed setting: 125 ISO

Viewfinder display

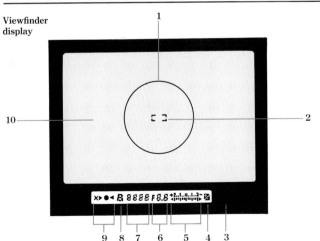

1 12mm-diameter central area
2 Focus brackets
3 Ready-light LED
4 Exposure compensation mark
5 Electronic analog display
6 Aperture/exposure compensation value
7 Shutter speed/film speed
8 Exposure mode
9 Focus indicators
10 Clear matte field

Electronic cameras ☐ 3

The Nikon F4 is the state-of-the-art electronic camera—the ultimate professional body that offers everything technology can do. The latest in the line that includes the FM2, F2 and F3, it incorporates many of their advantages as well as new features.

With a body of solid die-cast aluminium alloy, the F4 is rugged and built to withstand the toughest conditions. The body has a rubberized outer skin to make it shower safe and external levers and dials have been designed to keep out moisture and dust.

At the camera's heart are three microcomputers, which control systems such as metering and focusing. While the F4 does have autofocus, this is just one of many important features—a tool to be used when required, overridden when not. The autofocus system is extremely sensitive and can operate in light levels as low as EV-1, the equivalent of less than one candle.

The F4 also offers computerized focus tracking for subjects moving in a consistent manner. It can track the moving subject, anticipate where it will be at the time of exposure and preset the focus accordingly. It has three metering systems—spot, centre-weighted and matrix—for which the information from 100,000 images has been programmed into the camera (see pp. 32–33). The motor drive is built in and operates at a speed of 5.7 frames a second. A silent, but slower, speed can also be selected.

Canon, Minolta and other manufacturers also offer top-of-the-range professional cameras with similar features to the F4.

Remember, though, that technology doesn't guarantee a good picture unless the user knows how to handle it.

The Nikon TW Zoom is a sophisticated compact with a 35–80mm power zoom lens. Features include fully automatic film operation, autofocus, which operates even in low light levels, and built-in flash. The flash fires when selected or automatically in low light. An LCD panel displays all shooting information. Focus lock and exposure compensation options allow more creative choice than with earlier compacts.

The Minolta Weathermatic has a sealed body, giving it a greater resistance to water and dust than other compacts. Its robust construction makes it ideal for use on the beach, for example, or anywhere else a camera might get rough treatment.

Like all compacts, it has built-in flash, which is reliable but tends to be hard and direct and not very flattering. As a snapshot camera, however, this is one of the best.

Compacts

Compact 35mm cameras are light, easy to carry and offer a wide range of automatic features. They are simple to use and do not require the understanding of technology demanded by the electronic SLRs. A compact is the ideal family camera, good for slipping in the bag when going out for the day or on holiday. It will record the moments you want to remember with the minimum of fuss.

Despite all their advantages, however, compacts cannot match the versatility and creative possibilities offered by an SLR. Although some compacts have their own integral zoom this does not compete with the huge array of lens options in an SLR system which give the photographer so much more choice in picture-making. But, within their limits, compacts achieve satisfactory results and provide pictures that trigger memories and give much pleasure. Compacts are good cameras to use at social gatherings and, since they are totally automatic, excellent for nighttime photography.

17

Special purpose cameras

Although SLR camera systems fulfil most picture-taking requirements, there are occasions when a different type of camera might be employed for specific purposes. While the studio cameraman might specify a different larger format, there is also a range of other 35mm cameras designed for particular situations or pictures.

Nikonos V

Widelux
A portable camera designed for landscapes, this is also useful for making portraits of large groups. During an exposure the 26mm lens moves within its mount, describing an arc of 140°, and produces a sharp panoramic image occupying one and a half times the width of a normal 35mm frame. It has a limited range of shutter speeds (1/15, 1/60, 1/250 second). Use a pistol grip to help keep hands from intruding into the picture.

Nikonos
A rugged, all-purpose camera which can be taken underwater down to a depth of 50m (165ft). It can be fitted with any of five interchangeable lenses. Its unique construction features an inner body, which is sealed into the outer casing. Dustproof and virtually indestructible, it can be used in any environment from desert to mountains and in adverse conditions such as rain and sea spray.

Widelux

Leica
The quietest full-size 35mm camera —it is a non-reflex design without the noise-making mirror action common to SLRs. The design has remained virtually unchanged since its introduction in the 1920s. It is ruggedly constructed and extremely versatile. An extensive range of superior quality interchangeable lenses allows exposures to be made under any conditions, particularly when the light level is low. Many early masterpieces were taken on Leicas.

Leica M3

Minox

The smallest full-frame camera presently available. It has autofocus, accurate totally automatic aperture and shutter control and the fixed lens can produce an image of high enough quality for press reproduction. Due to its pocket size and reliable mechanism it can be carried at all times and is suited to candid and spontaneous photography.

Minox

Olympus SuperZoom 300

The Olympus SuperZoom 300 This camera is designed to be operated with one hand. The user can slip a hand through the side strap and reach the shutter button. A rangefinder camera, it offers all the latest technology, such as autofocus, programmed autoexposure and built-in flash. The 38–105mm lens automatically retracts when power is turned off.

Kodak Panorama

Kodak Weekend 35

Disposable cameras come ready loaded with film and cannot be re-used. Different makes offer features such as flash and wider than usual prints. There is even an underwater version, the Kodak Weekend 35, which can be used in depths of 3.5m (12ft) of water.

Fujicolor Flash

Lenses ☐ I

The selection of a lens is one of the most important creative decisions the photographer has to make. The shorter the focal length the greater is its angle of view; conversely, the longer the focal length the narrower the angle of view. The focal length of the lens also affects the relative image size of the subject.

An important characteristic of a lens is its effect on perspective. Wide angles exaggerate perspective, while long focus lenses foreshorten. Similarly, depth of field—distance between foreground and background—is much greater on wide angle lenses than telephotos. An understanding of these basic optical principles will make you a more creative photographer.

When choosing the lens in which to frame a picture, be aware not only of the shape of the subject, but also of the other shapes created between the frame and subject. Do not look only at the subject in the viewfinder; look at the complete picture.

To become a "natural" photographer try framing pictures in the mind's eye—whether or not the eye is behind a camera viewfinder.

With experience a camera user will come to know instinctively which properties of which group of lenses will best enhance the picture. Many professional photographers use a particular lens so frequently that it becomes their identifiable style.

In addition to general purpose lenses, a number of specialist types are produced. Zoom, macro, superfast and ultra-wide angle lenses are now available for all cameras; many of these are autofocus. Optical technology has advanced so much that it is now cheaper to produce an autofocus lens than an old-style manual focus lens.

Get to know your lenses: it is as important to become familiar with a new lens as with a new car. The balance of a lens in the hand, the position and operation of its controls and its optical characteristics are the key factors.

Fisheye 8mm f2.8
(angle of view 180°)
Fisheyes were originally designed to photograph cloud cover for meteorologists. The wide angle of view and circular frame can contain a complete horizontal plane when photographing directly upward or downward. The extreme distortion limits their use and makes fisheyes unsuitable for most general photography.

15mm f5.6 (angle of view 110°)
An ultra-wide angle lens with little image distortion—it doesn't bend the vertical or horizontal lines. It has enormous depth of field capability and doesn't really need to be focused unless used close up. Because of its extreme exaggeration of perspective, spectacular pictures can be made; a fine lens for interiors and sweeping landscapes. Filters must be used on the back of the lens.

20mm f2.8 (angle of view 94°)
The most popular ultra-wide angle lens with many professional photographers, the 20mm is extremely versatile. Like the 15mm, it is good for interiors and dynamic pictures, but comes into its own for landscapes when used with polarizing filters. Graphic compositions can be made which utilize exaggeration of perspective without appearing gimmicky.

24mm f2.8 autofocus
(angle of view 84°)
A versatile lens and the widest that can take more than two filters without vignetting. It provides just enough distortion without the image flying off the sides. The wide aperture makes it a good lens for using in crowds or tight areas. The photographer can stand back to frame a group but still maintain close contact.

Lenses □ 2

35mm f1.4 (angle of view 62°)

Although a wide angle, the 35mm should be the 35mm photographer's standard lens. Its angle of view and minimal distortion allow more possibilities for composition than a normal lens. When shooting people, this lens emphasizes the relationship between subject and environment. The ability to get "inside" a picture creates an intimacy between photographer and subject.

50mm f1.4 autofocus (angle of view 46°)

The 50mm lens is universally known as "normal" because it corresponds to the angle of view of the human eye. It usually has the largest aperture in any range. If possible, select the one with the largest aperture from the several choices of 50mm lens. This lens is used when a photographer is working in low light levels or wants no perspective distortion.

85mm f1.8 (angle of view 28°)

This is a popular focal length with professional photographers for studio portraits and general reportage. It comes in a range of maximum apertures: the 2.8 is very light while the 1.4 is big and heavy but produces images of excellent quality. However, fixed focal length lenses, such as the 85mm, have been superseded by zoom lenses.

105mm f2.8 (angle of view 23°)

One of the finest focal lengths for 35mm cameras, the 105mm is a favourite of all professionals. Photographers consider it an ideal portrait lens because, when fully framing a head, it photographs the face as the mind's eye sees it, with no distortion. It is sharp and fast, an ideal lens for hand holding.

There are many lenses of focal lengths in between the ones described here. The examples shown are an indication of the optical properties and applications of a cross section of useful lenses, not a catalogue of all available types.

Lenses are often considered as belonging to specific families—such as wide angle or telephoto—and useful for certain designated subjects. However, this is not necessarily always so. Good portraits can be taken on ultra-wide angle lenses; architectural subjects can be shot on telephotos as long as the photographer is aware of the level of distortion and the effect on perspective.

There are big price differences between lens ranges, but as a rule you get what you pay for. Some ranges, such as Vivitar Series 1, are excellent, but most cheap lenses are of poorer quality.

If the price of a new lens is beyond reach, secondhand lenses by a good system manufacturer such as Nikon or Canon are excellent value. Even if a used lens is out of adjustment it can often be reset at reasonable cost.

Always test a used lens before purchase. Photograph a flat, textured surface, such as a brick wall, at various apertures. Project the picture or enlarge it as much as possible and scrutinize the edges for fall-off or distortion. If the image appears sharp from edge to edge the lens is in good condition.

There are some lenses with specific technical applications. Among lenses designed for medical and technical purposes is the Medical-Nikkor, a close-focusing lens with built-in ring flash. The Endoscope fibre optic lens is an attachment which transmits light from inaccessible areas to the lens. It is used in medical work to photograph the inside of the body, and in engineering to analyze the interior of engines.

The 2000mm catadioptric (mirror) lens is the longest telephoto made. It is used mainly for astronomy and surveillance and offers magnification 40 times that of a normal lens.

Lenses □ 3

180mm f2.8 (angle of view 13°)

With its wide aperture the 180mm was a popular semi-telelens but has now been superseded by zooms such as the 80–200mm. 180mm is a useful and versatile focal length, however. It is excellent for colour reportage work, presenting a good relationship between subject and background—a good lens for shooting people across the street.

300mm f4.5 autofocus (angle of view 8°)

This is the first of the real telephoto lenses; it sees closer than the human eye does. It compresses perspective with minimal depth of focus, providing exciting picture possibilities. Because of its light weight, it is the standard telephoto lens for press and sports work, allowing the photographer to stand well away from the subject.

300mm f2.8 IF ED autofocus (angle of view 8°)

A professional lens which gives excellent picture quality. IF means internal focus; ED refers to a coating on the lens which gives better colour rendition and stops flare. This 300 is the standard press photographer's lens, heavy but manageable and usually used with a monopod. It is also popular for outdoor fashion.

600mm f4 (angle of view 4°)

Visual and technical precision are vital when using this lens. It must nearly always be used with a tripod or monopod for static pictures but "panning" is possible. The compression of perspective and shallow depth of field that it achieves can give extraordinary and exciting results. The lens also enables pictures to be taken of subjects that are physically inaccessible.

The **relationship of subject to** background is illustrated in these pictures, taken on three different lenses. The couple were in the same positions for each picture.

The 20mm lens exaggerates the difference between the couple and background.

For this shot on a 135mm lens the photographer moved back from the subjects but the buildings appear to be closer to them.

For this 600mm lens shot the photographer moved farther back. The couple now appear to be sitting very close to the buildings behind them.

Specialist lenses

Teleconverters are magnifying elements placed between the lens and the camera to increase focal length by × 2 or × 1.4 (shown here). Although useful for adapting an existing lens for telephoto use, they cut out light and demand an increase of f-stops. Teleconverters can, however, provide an exact focal length in a range where there is no manufactured lens. A 180mm, for example, can be converted to a 360mm lens.

15mm lens (angle of view 110°)

50mm lens (angle of view 46°)

Perspective correction lenses are used to correct the distortion of vertical or horizontal lines—particularly important when photographing buildings to stop them appearing to fall over backwards. Conversely, they can exaggerate such distortion for special effect. By offsetting the front of the lens a perspective corrector can also be used to simulate the effect of moving the camera. A 28mm f3.5 lens is shown here.

Macro lenses come in focal lengths of 60mm, 105mm and 200mm. They are used for close-up work, for photographing details or natural history subjects and also for copying drawings and artwork. Certain zoom lenses have a macro facility built in which can be selected when required. The macro shown here is a 60mm f2.8 autofocus which takes a life-size (1:1) image of the subject; some macros take a half life-size (1:2) image.

600mm lens (angle of view 4°)

Mirror lenses are so called because the passage of light within the lens is deflected by mirrors. Light enters the lens and travels to the back, where it hits a mirror and is reflected back onto another mirror at the front of the lens; from there the light is reflected back to the shutter. Mirror lenses are about half the size and weight of other lenses and thus easier to carry. They make out-of-focus highlights appear like doughnuts.

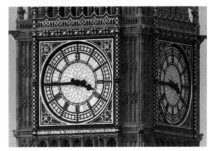

1200mm lens (angle of view 2°)

These views of Westminster, London were all taken from the same point. Note the size of the clock: the longer the focal length, the greater its magnification. Focal length also controls the picture angle: the longer the focal length used the narrower the picture angle.

27

Zoom lenses

A zoom lens is several lenses in one. It gives a choice of focal lengths, enabling variations of the same picture to be composed from the same position. The photographer can come in tight or pull back for a wider shot without moving. Once believed to be inferior to fixed focal length lenses, zoom lenses are now of excellent quality and actually cheaper to produce than ordinary lenses. Most top-of-the-range zooms now offer autofocus as well as manual.

Zooms increase your creative options at less cost than individual lenses—and you can change focal length more quickly. Another point well worth bearing in mind is that camera equipment is heavy and carrying two zoom lenses is much easier than having seven or eight individual lenses weighing you down. A 35–70mm and an 80–200mm cover all the most useful focal lengths other than a really wide angle. Don't buy a zoom lens with too great a focal length—a 24–200mm, for example. The construction cannot cope with such a range and the quality of the image suffers.

Use circular polarizing filters. Do not

35–70mm zoom

35–70mm zoom f3.5 autofocus (angle of view 62°–34°) The versatile 35–70mm covers the "normal" lens range and is an excellent first lens. It is good for portraits and has a macro facility.

Both shots of the snake charmer were taken on a 35–70mm zoom. The 35mm shot, *below left*, sets the man in his location in front of the Red Fort, Delhi. Man and building are of equal importance. The 70mm shot, *below right*, was taken without moving position, but from a lower viewpoint, and is much more a portrait of the snake charmer. The zoom has allowed the photographer to get close to his subject—without getting too near the snake.

use graduated filters with an autofocus zoom—the front element of the lens turns as it goes through the zoom and will cause the filter to affect the wrong part of the picture.

When a subject is approaching or moving away from the camera it is easy to hold focus and keep that subject full frame with a zoom.

80–200mm zoom

80–200mm zoom f2.8 autofocus (angle of view 30°–12°) The most useful long zoom lens, the 80–200mm is extremely sharp and manageable, holding focus throughout the zoom. Contrast can be increased by using a longer lens hood than the one supplied.

The 80–200mm zoom is the ideal lens to carry when out for the day. Both these pictures were taken on the zoom during a day in Oporto, Portugal.

The atmospheric portrait of the garlic seller was shot on 80mm, which works well for close-up detail.

At the other end of its range the lens is equally successful for the view of the city taken on 200mm. This focal length foreshortens the perspective and packs the buildings up to create a full frame. The wide aperture of this lens allows it to be hand held at fairly slow speeds when light conditions are not good.

Autofocus

Automatic focusing is a relatively recent SLR feature—the first SLR autofocus camera was introduced in 1985. Some photographers love it; others are suspicious. Autofocus is best thought of as just another tool, something that can be extremely useful in certain situations but not to be trusted implicitly. Get to know its strengths and weaknesses.

One advantage of autofocus is that, with this important task taken care of, the photographer can concentrate more on the framing and composition of the picture. It is ideal for taking subjects that dart around a lot, such as young children and animals, and for sport and oncoming subjects. It is superior to manual focusing in low light levels and can even operate in darkness.

Autofocus can take up to a couple of seconds to operate. In order not to lose your picture while waiting for autofocus get into the habit of pushing the button in two stages. Press lightly to engage autofocus and keep your finger on the button. Once the subject is sharp, wait for the expression or action you want before pressing down fully to take the picture.

Since the focusing brackets are in the centre of the viewfinder autofocus may not succeed in getting an off-centre subject sharp. Frame the subject of the photograph in the centre of the viewfinder, operate the autofocus lock button and reframe as required.

Autofocus usually operates in two modes: single and continuous. In the latter mode, autofocus can follow a subject moving in a continuous repeating pattern and keep it in focus; you can then shoot whenever you like.

Autofocus works well for oncoming subjects. These horses were heading directly toward the camera and fill the frame with action. Autofocus held them sharp as they approached, enabling a few frames to be shot before they came too close.

The constant bobbing movements of small animals such as marmosets make them difficult subjects to photograph, but autofocus eases the problem. For this picture, taken on an 80–200mm zoom at 1/500 second, the autofocus brackets on the viewing screen were centred on the animal's eyes. Focus held while the animal moved around. The fast shutter speed was necessary to freeze the action.

Young children can present much the same problem as the marmoset and are also good subjects for autofocus. These two were so excited by their Christmas presents that it was impossible to keep them still, but autofocus held them sharp.

Autofocus does not work well when there are two subjects, each to one side of the frame. It focuses not on the people but on the centre of the picture—in this instance the irrelevant buildings, *left*. To solve this problem, frame one of the subjects, lock the autofocus, recompose and shoot. The subjects of the picture are then sharp against a blurred background, *right*.

Exposure □ I

Photography is to do with light—the understanding of it and the correct photographic use of it. The highly sophisticated metering systems of the latest electronic cameras will solve most of the problems for you—and do it very well—but the photographer still needs to know the limitations of the camera's "expertise" and when and why to override it.

There are three basic types of metering which the photographer can select: matrix or evaluated, centre weighted and spot.

The system known as matrix in Nikon cameras, evaluative in Canon, is the most sophisticated. The picture is split into five or six segments. Each of these is then evaluated so the camera can decide on exposure. The metering computer has been programmed in such a way that it can make creative decisions; it recognizes if a subject is backlit, if there are strong highlights or if the subject is a small, brightly lit area.

This is possible because the computer has been programmed with analyses of the subject matter and exposure levels of some 100,000 photographs. By using this stored experience the camera can make a sound decision on the correct exposure for a given picture.

In the centre-weighted system the meter concentrates 60 or 75 percent (depending on the camera model) of its sensitivity in the centre of the viewfinder. The balance is "feathered" out toward the edges. The advantage of this method is that it gives the photographer more control, more flexibility. The camera can be moved around to meter different areas of the picture and the photographer makes the final decision.

In spot metering the reading is taken from a central circle about 5mm in diameter—about 2.5 percent of the viewfinder area. A precise reading can thus be taken off any area of the photograph. Spot metering is ideal for use in difficult light conditions or when the important element in the picture is small—a detail or the subject's face.

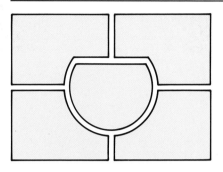

Matrix metering splits the picture into five segments in order to judge optimum overall exposure.

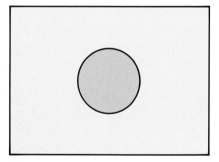

Centre-weighted metering concentrates the bulk of its sensitivity on a 12mm central area of the viewfinder.

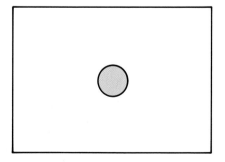

Spot metering takes a precise reading from a 5mm diameter circle.

Sunset pictures are ideal candidates for matrix metering. Using its stored "experience" of such pictures the camera can recognize that the sun is not important and expose for the general scene. Each section is evaluated separately so the sun does not disrupt the reading. Without matrix the meter would have exposed for the bright sun and the rest of the picture would have been underexposed.

In this daylight portrait of Hungarian pianist Zoltan Kochas the subject is surrounded by dark furniture and white walls, making correct exposure problematic. With centre-weighted metering the reading was taken from the central dark areas, ignoring the white walls. Both the key elements, face and piano, are perfectly exposed in the resulting picture.

A shaft of very strong daylight lit this monk, standing in a dark monastery. In order to expose for the brightly lit face spot metering was used to take a precise reading off an area of the face.

This dramatic effect could only really have been achieved with the pinpoint accuracy of spot metering and emphasizes the importance of choosing the correct metering mode for the picture.

Exposure □ 2

There is no such thing as correct exposure—only the exposure for the picture you want to take. The camera is just a tool in the photographer's hands; despite all the technological innovations it has no taste.

Exposure can make or break a picture, but the right level for the picture is not always what the meter says. Older cameras without sophisticated metering systems often give too general a reading. This can be acceptable for evenly lit subjects, but may cause problems when there is a great difference in light levels. Even when using electronic metering

systems there are areas which require bracketing and special care:

1 With wide angle lenses when the quantity of sky in the picture may have too much influence on the reading.

2 When using two or more filters, especially polarizing filters.

3 With high speed film such as 1600 ISO and above; the film is not as fast as it claims and can be underexposed.

4 When taking pictures with high contrast and subjects not in centre (see examples, *right*).

Bracketing
Using bracketing as a technique enables a photographer to explore all exposure possibilities and make certain of getting the desired shot. Pictures may be obtained that even the most experienced photographer might not have expected. There are four ways of bracketing:

Varying the f-stop
The first method, *above*, is to change the f-stop from the one indicated by the meter. Under most light conditions this means taking a frame at the metered aperture, then one at a half stop under, and another at a half stop over. In low light levels or when using slow shutter speeds try going as much as two stops each side of the indicated aperture. This can also be

useful when working in unfamiliar light conditions.

Some electronic cameras make a mechanical exposure at about 1/100 second when the batteries are run down. In this instance f-stop bracketing is the only way to alter exposure. The new electronic cameras do not work at all if batteries are exhausted.

Shutter speed
If aperture priority is critical to maintain depth of field, bracket by varying the shutter speed. At a fixed f-stop one frame is taken at the indicated shutter speed, then one above and one below that. For example, if the indicated shutter speed is 1/125 second, try another frame at 1/60 second and a third at 1/250 second. (On

An off-centre black cat in snow presents an extreme exposure problem. Take an incident light reading or a camera reading off neutral grey, such as your hand, and bracket to overexpose. Alternatively take a spot reading from the cat and bracket.

For a light subject on a dark background—a white cat on a pile of coal—do exactly the same but bracket to underexpose. On automatic, the result would probably be a ghostly cat, with no detail, amid overexposed coal.

On the bracketed frames, *above,* exposure was varied by two stops: from f5.6, for the face and coat, to f11, for the building. Of the resulting pictures the girl appears at her best in frame 21, the buildings in frame 25. The final choice of frame must depend on what was important in the picture.

electronic cameras shutters work at speeds in between those shown on the dial.)

ISO setting
A third method of bracketing is by changing the film speed setting. When using 200 ISO film, for example, shoot one frame at the correct setting; change the dial to 150 ISO (half a stop over) for the second, and then to 300 ISO (half a stop under). The photographer must be very familiar with the camera to use this method successfully.

Neutral density filters
The fourth method of bracketing uses neutral density filters to cut down the light; the camera must be on manual. Use two filters, an ND1, which cuts light by half a stop, and an ND2, which cuts light by one stop. Shoot the first frame with the ND1, the next with no filter, and the third with the ND2. The basic reading is taken with the ND1 on the lens.

This method allows the use of a particular shutter and aperture combination in an uncontrollable light source. In bright sunlight, for instance, use of ND filters is the only way to maintain a wide aperture.

Aperture and shutter

A camera is a box with a lens at one side and film holder at the other. The camera contains a shutter; the lens has an iris. Light enters the camera through the lens and exposes the film when the shutter is opened.

The iris is a system of metal leaves which can open and close. The space in the middle is the aperture, the size of which is measured in f-stops. The aperture governs the volume of light landing on the film; the shutter controls the length of time that light is allowed to land on the film. If the shutter speed is doubled, the amount of light is halved. This is also the effect if the size of the aperture is decreased by one stop. Conversely, a wider aperture or slower shutter lets more light through.

Correct exposure is obtained when the aperture and shutter speed are in the right relationship, governed by what speed of film is being used. The exposure meter needle moves with fluctuations of light

Stopped down—a small aperture holds focus from foreground to background. Bracket shutter speeds. The picture, *below*, was taken with an exposure of f22 at ¼ second on a 35mm lens.

A wide open aperture creates an out-of-focus background with no unnecessary detail intruding on the flower subject, *above*. Shot on an 85mm lens at f2, with an exposure of 1/1000 second.

and indicates a range of shutter/aperture combinations, any of which are technically correct.

Aperture determines the depth of field—how sharp the picture is in front and behind the point on which the lens is focused; the smaller the aperture the greater the depth of field. With the lens wide open only the point of focus is sharp. A scale on the lens barrel indicates the extent of the area in focus at each aperture. The effects of aperture control are most visible on long lenses.

The preview button on the camera enables the stopped-down image to be seen. Make it a habit to use this to check sharpness. If more depth of field is wanted, use a slower shutter and a tripod.

The shutter controls the effect of movement by the subject in the picture. It will either freeze the action or give the impression of movement. With modern cameras there is an infinitely variable range of shutter speeds.

Slow shutter speeds can convey movement. The waterfall, *above*, was photographed at a shutter speed of about 1 second with the camera securely mounted on a tripod.

Fast shutter speeds freeze action to make a dramatic picture. The horse, *below*, was captured frozen in mid-air at the moment of the jump by using a shutter speed of 1/2000 second.

Exposure meters

Although camera metering is sophisticated, the serious photographer should not be without a good independent meter. With this, the level of light in every relevant area of the picture can be ascertained—often difficult and slow to work out with built-in meters.

As with camera meters, the hand meter only provides basic information. The photographer then has to apply this to the individual picture requirements.

There is no guarantee that any meter will give the exposure for the perfect picture, but intelligent use of the camera meter and the hand meter, combined with bracketing, should result in correct exposures.

Study any mistakes. If a note is kept of exposure details, much can be learned from bad pictures.

Grey card readings
Most scenes, when reduced to monotones, represent about 18 percent grey. Film speeds and camera and TTL meters are calibrated for this average tone (reproduced on p.240).

Other 18 percent grey areas are grass, trees, tarmacadam, dull brickwork and neutral-coloured clothing. For correct exposure in non-average conditions, measure something that represents this grey tone. When using ultra-wide angle lenses, determine the exposure off the ground, then recompose the picture using that exposure reading.

The Lunasix (Luna Pro) is one of the most versatile of all meters. The basic unit is an accurate available light meter, capable of reading from extremely low light levels up to the brightest daylight.

Flash meters work on an incident light principle, measuring the amount of light falling on the subject.

The Minolta IV is a remote meter which does not have to be plugged into the flash unit (no trailing wires or cables). It can be used with hand flash or large studio units and as a daylight meter. It measures from the lowest light levels through to midday sky.

The Weston Euro-Master is a selenium meter and useful for most general purposes. Since it is not battery powered it is good for use in extreme cold or high humidity, where batteries are unreliable. It is less sensitive in low-lit areas.

Lunasix (Luna Pro)

Minolta IV

Weston Euro-Master

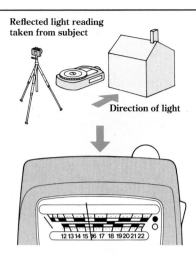

Reflected light reading taken from subject

Direction of light

Incident reading taken with diffuser in place

Direction of light

12 13 14 15 16 17 18 19 20 21 22

12 13 14 15 16 17 18 19 20 21 22

Hand held meters can be used in two different ways to measure either reflected or incident light.

Reflected light readings are taken from the light which bounces off the subject in the direction of the lens. This is much the same as taking a reading with the camera meter, although the hand meter is more versatile.

Incident light readings are those where the meter is held in front of the subject but facing the light source, so measuring the amount of light falling on it. To take these readings the meter must have a light diffuser; the Minolta IV is a good example. Incident readings give a more accurate interpretation of the light falling on the subject without being affected by the brightness of the subject.

Once the film speed has been set, and an exposure value indicated on the scale, the complete range of relevant shutter/aperture combinations becomes evident.

Colour temperature meters measure the "colour" of light and indicate the type of filtration required to achieve a correct colour balance for the film in use. They are mainly used when photographing in mixed light conditions with transparency film.

Spot meters are used for precision work. They have a reflex viewing system with a spot in the middle of the screen which takes a one degree measurement. Readings can be taken of all areas of the picture from a considerable distance, providing the photographer with sufficient information from which to expose correctly for any part of the picture. Spot meters are ideal for photographing backlit subjects, sport and stage performers.

Pentax spot meter

Minolta colour meter

39

Film □ transparency

There are many types of transparency (slide) film on the market, most available all over the world.

Daylight film is colour balanced for noon/daylight, electronic flash and blue flashbulbs. Other films are balanced for tungsten (inside light) of various types. Use filters to balance the colour of light for the film.

Film is available in various speeds rated from 25 to 3200. The rating refers to the sensitivity of the film to light: the higher the rating, the faster or more sensitive the film. The faster films are inevitably coarser in grain and less sharp. Most transparency film is now processed by the E6 system. All E6 films are best processed soon after exposure.

Kodachrome films use a different processing system (K14) which the user cannot employ. Stable and an excellent film for use on long trips, Kodachrome film has a quality that can make a picture—the picture of Whitby harbour, *right*, was shot on Kodachrome 64, an excellent film.

Fastidious photographers choose films by batches, since each batch of film can vary slightly. Check the information sheet enclosed with the film to make sure it corresponds with ISO marked on the pack. (ISO is now the standard international rating and has replaced previous ASA and DIN rating systems.)

Saturation is a term used to describe density and strength of colour. With many films, slight underexposure will increase saturation. Many professionals overrate transparency film. A 25 ISO, for example, can be shot at 32; 64 ISO at 80. The slightly underexposed transparency ensures saturated colour.

Kodachrome 25. Daylight. Sharpest and least grainy ordinary slide film available. Stable but slow. Colours less saturated than Ektachrome. Good exposure latitude.

Kodachrome 64. Daylight. Slightly higher contrast than Kodachrome 25 but virtually the same sharpness and grain. Good all-round film; filtration improves skin tones.

Fujichrome 50D. Fine grain with good, sharp edge detail. Warm skin tones. Good for portraits and landscapes. Sharp from foreground to background but needs a tripod.

Agfachrome 50RS. Extremely sharp. Realistic skin tones. Soft tonal rendition. Warmer than Kodachrome and Fujichrome. Good beauty film.

Ektachrome 64. A favourite ISO of professional photographers. True colour and performs well in all conditions. Slow for hand holding unless in good light.

Fujichrome 100D. General purpose film. All colours appear bright. Natural warm tones. Good in studio and outdoors. Be careful with skin tones when using 81A filters.

Agfachrome 100RS. Sharp, accurate colour rendition and good tonal separation. Good for beauty and a kind portrait film. E6 process.

Ektachrome 100. Excellent skin tones and primary colours, especially reds. Sharper than Ektachrome 64. Does not have very good latitude.

Kodachrome 200. Needs uprating by a third of a stop when using matrix or similar metering. Good shadow rendition but loses detail in highlights when overexposed.

Ektachrome 200. Daylight. Good for general use. Clean separation of subtle hues. For good colour rate at 250 ISO. Process normal.

 Fujichrome 400D. Good colour saturation and wide latitude. Handles mixed lighting well. Good contrast even when pushed to 800 ISO. Ideal for reportage.

 Scotch Chrome 1000. Good for soft pastel colours. Grainy film, gives painterly effect. Very flattering when used with a soft focus filter.

 Agfachrome 1000RS. Ultra-fast emulsion for shooting in very low light. Good soft grain. E6 process.

 Fujichrome 1600D. Can be pushed to 3200 but best rated at 1600, when colours are most consistent. Warm yellow-biased tones; the more it is pushed the yellower it appears.

 Polaroid Polachrome 35mm. Instant pictures if you carry the autoprocessor. Quality unlike any other transparency film. A very useful aid.

 Ektachrome 50. Artificial light version of Ektachrome 64. Excellent film for still life—long exposures create minimal reciprocity failure. Wonderful for reds. E6 process. Uprates successfully.

 Ektachrome 160. Balanced for artificial light. Good for interior work and stage lighting. Expose for the highlights. Do not push more than two stops.

 Scotch Chrome 640-T. Fastest tungsten light-balanced film on the market. Very grainy but good in domestic and studio lighting. Expose for the highlights. Pushes well.

 Ektachrome Infrared. Special film sensitive to IR and visible spectrum. Bracket exposures and take care with focusing. A film to experiment with.

 Agfa Dia Direct. 32 ISO. The only monochrome slide film. Gives excellent results with pleasant warm-black colour. Expose carefully. Requires special processing.

41

Film □ black and white

There are two approaches to shooting black and white pictures. Either shoot a perfect negative from which to obtain a great print, or just shoot to get the picture and adjust the result in the processing. In both instances the initial exposure dictates how the film should be developed and what type of print is suitable.

To get the best from black and white a photographer needs a darkroom and specialist knowledge which can only be touched on here. When choosing black and white film be sure to select the right film for the intended picture.

Slow film (25–50 ISO)

These films have extremely fine grain, but must be developed accurately to obtain optimum quality. Good definition is achieved either when shot in bright light or when long exposures can be made. Its ability to record a wide range of tones is useful with subjects such as architecture.

Medium film (100–125 ISO)

This range of films has a fair amount of latitude—the ability to cope with many different light conditions—and can be pushed if required. At its normal speed rating it is best used when the light level is bright—in summer sunshine, or under studio lighting. Its slower speed allows the photographer to vary the f-stops to a greater degree than with fast film.

Fast film (400–3200 ISO)

News and reportage photographers choose fast film for its wide latitude. When shot at its normal rated speed it has good grain structure. It can be pushed three f-stops or more and can be processed in many types of developer, depending on the negative quality required.

Kids on a San Francisco street were photographed on a 35mm lens using Tri-X 400. An extremely reliable and high quality film, Kodak Tri-X is the standard against which other black and white film is judged.

Agfapan APX25. Professional film. Fine grain and good definition but slower than some comparable types without excessive contrast.

Ilford Pan F. 50 ISO. Extremely fine grain, high contrast and very sharp. An excellent choice of slow film for general photography.

Agfapan APX100. Professional film. Almost as sharp as Agfapan 25 despite speed increase, but has coarser grain.

Kodak Plus-X pan 125. Good grain and definition. A reasonable general purpose film with no unusual characteristics.

Kodak T-Max 100. Flat, angular T-grain crystals in this film give greater sharpness. Needs to be carefully developed in its own developer.

Ilford FP4. 125 ISO. Considered by many to be the best of the medium speed monochrome films for general photography.

Agfapan 400. Professional film. Best rated at 300, especially indoors or with artificial lighting. Reasonable sharpness, considering speed. Good grain.

Kodak Tri-X pan 400. Grain and definition good. One of the two best films in terms of grain/speed/sharpness ratios. Suitable for push processing.

Kodak T-Max 400. T-grain crystals said to give sharper appearance and fine grain to picture. Develop with care to maintain separation.

Ilford HP5. 400 ISO. Similar to Tri-X although not identical. Suitable for push processing. One of the two best films in this group.

Fuji Neopan 400. Fine grain. Good for shadow detail without losing highlight detail. Performs best at ISO 400 and 800.

Fuji Neopan 1600. Like the 400 this is popular for newspaper work because of its high contrasts and short development time.

Kodak T-Max 3200. Ultra-sensitive film producing high quality results in dimly lit situations. Can be pushed up to five stops.

Agfaortho 25. Document copying film. High quality prints when meticulously processed in Agfa chemicals. Use instant light reading or grey card for correct exposure.

Kodak Recording Film. 1000 ISO but generally expose at 1600 ISO. Made for surveillance work in dim light. Increased sensitivity to red.

Kodak High Speed Infrared Film. For pictorial work use a red filter and rate 50 ISO. Set lens by IR index. Read instructions! Coarse grain and high contrast.

Kodak technical pan. Slowest film on the market—10 ISO. Allows good enlargement up to 60 times. Kodak Technidol LC developer.

Ilford XPI400. The universal black and white film. Good contrast range. Fine grain, however, for a fast film. C41 process.

Black and white photography is a medium in its own right—it is not simply taking colour subjects in monochrome. Most reportage and fine art photographers find shooting with colour distracting and prefer the tonal subtlety and directness of the black and white print.

Film □ colour negative

Colour negative films range in speed from 25–1600 ISO and use the Kodak C41 processing system or equivalent. They are universal in balance and can be used in all types of lighting and colour corrected at printing stage.

Like transparency film, colour negative is easily damaged and needs careful handling. Good prints will only come from good quality negatives. There is a huge choice of processing labs for colour negative film, and mini-labs offering a one-hour service have sprung up in every station and shopping area in recent years. Results are usually adequate, but always ask yourself whether you really need the prints in an hour or can wait a little longer and spend less.

Kodak Ektar 25. Finest colour film. Very slow and virtually grain free. Good for detail and ideal for enlargements. Good colour saturation.

Kodacolor Gold 100. Slightly warm colours with good tonal range. Uniform grain and good exposure latitude. A suitable film for use with compacts.

Agfacolor XRS 100. Good primary colours and improved sharpness. Skin tones more neutral than Kodak. Slightly faster than 100 ISO.

Fujicolor Reala 100. Colours extremely realistic if printed well. Excellent for skin tones and for use in mixed light.

Kodak Ektar 125. Sharper grain than Kodacolor Gold and less contrasty. Warm flesh tones. Kodak claim it can be stored for 50–100 years.

Kodak Vericolor III. Rate at 125 ISO. Good for overall detail. Designed for exposures of 1/10 second or less.

Agfacolor XRS 200. Good neutral colour film with satisfactory shadow detail and vibrant primary colours. Extremely wide latitude.

Fujicolor 200. Similar to Fujicolor 100 but faster and with slight loss in colour saturation. Good film for use with compact cameras.

Agfacolor XRS 400. Like Agfa 200 can be under- or over-exposed. Good film for use with compacts with slow zoom lenses.

Fujicolor 400. Good fine grain. Designed specifically for the postcard-size print market. Suitable for use in low light conditions.

Kodak Ektapress 400. Professional film designed for modern newspaper technology. Acceptable colours; quick to process.

Kodak Ektar 1000. Excellent grain for such fast film and acceptable colours. Overall performance compares well with 400 ISO film.

Agfacolor XRS 1000. Wide latitude holds all detail in contrasty low lighting. Can produce atmospheric pictures in poor light. Hand print.

Kodak Ektapress 1600. Kodak's fastest colour film, designed for push processing. Increased blue tones when pushed. Pronounced grain.

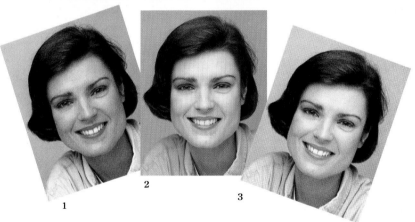

1

2

3

One-hour processing

More and more people take their colour negative film to one-hour processing labs. While results are generally good, remember that prints do not receive individual attention. Film is batched, put through a film processor and printed onto a continuous roll of paper. Prints are then cut by machine and sorted. All receive the same treatment; if film needs more attention, take it to a specialist laboratory.

Of these test prints the harbour scene, *top*, photographed on Kodak 125 Ektar has been well reproduced and colours are good and bright. A good negative shot in bright, even light and with no one dominant colour, this should not have presented any problems to a processor.

The portrait results are more variable. Skin tones are much too magenta in the print **(1)** and too green in **(2)**; only print **(3)** is acceptable.

Film □ handling

All film materials deteriorate with time; colour film is especially affected by temperature and humidity. If changes in climatic conditions occur, the speed and colour balance of film is likely to undergo some alteration.

There are two types of colour film; one is designed for professional use, the other for amateurs. Professional film is of extremely high quality and more consistent roll for roll than amateur, but has a shorter shelf life. For best results manufacturers advise that professional film should be stored in stable conditions at temperatures of 13°C (55°F) or below and processed soon after use.

Film intended for extremely critical colour reproduction should be kept in a freezer at even lower temperatures, around − 20°C (− 4°F). Before use allow the film to return to room temperature—slowly to avoid condensation inside the cassette. Process film as soon as possible after use.

Amateur film has a longer shelf life, remains more stable under varying conditions and has a more general application than professional film. It is designed for less critical applications. Manufacturers assume that amateur film will be stored at room temperature and the length of time between purchase and process will be longer than with professional films.

Adverse conditions

When travelling in hot countries use amateur film for its greater stability. If kept under the same controlled conditions as professional film the consistency of amateur film batches can be maintained.

Film is packaged in sealed foil and airtight cans to protect it from humidity. Under humid conditions process exposed film as quickly as possible.

On location keep exposed film separate from unexposed rolls and protect it just as carefully. Once packs are opened they must be protected from light. Never open a film pack until it is to be loaded.

Insulated bags (see pp.74–75) are use-

ful for carrying film; in hot weather, put a freezer sachet in the bag to keep temperatures low.

Exceptionally cold conditions are as bad for film as heat. It is likely to crack or snap and may also cut the fingers when being handled.

Chemicals and radiation are other dangers from which film must be protected. X-ray scanners used in airport security can damage unprocessed film. Lead-lined bags offer some protection, but, to be sure, try and arrange for film to bypass the X-ray. Ask for a hand check.

The range and availability of films changes rapidly. Try and ensure that you have the right film for the task in hand. In theory a long exposure made in daylight should provide a picture equivalent to one

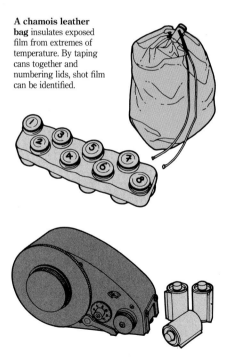

A chamois leather bag insulates exposed film from extremes of temperature. By taping cans together and numbering lids, shot film can be identified.

Use of a bulk loader enables photographers to save on the cost of film. Available in 30.5m (100ft) lengths, the film is wound onto used cassettes. Bulk loaders are essential for use with motor drive back units.

CHECKPOINTS

● Only push (uprate the speed) when it is the only way to make the exposure.

● Rate film slower than indicated in tungsten or low light levels.

● Expose for shadow details—never starve a negative film of light. Even when film is pushed, shadow detail will not improve. A flat light on a subject enables detail to be extracted from pushed film.

● Even under low light levels, an image usually registers on black and white film. If a scene is visible it can be photographed, but it may need an exposure of 30 minutes or more.

● Orthochromatic films are blind to red and yellow. They are used for copying when no mid-tones are required.

● Films for general use are panchromatic—sensitive to all colours.

● To see how colour tones convert to monochrome adjust the controls of a colour television set to black and white.

● Modern film emulsions have a long life. Manufacturers claim that, properly stored, transparencies and negatives should remain in good condition for a hundred years.

made at a shorter exposure in bright light. In fact there is an area at both ends of the exposure range where film emulsions behave inconsistently.

In extremely long exposures under dim light, or very short ones under bright light, films can appear underexposed; with colour film the balance of one of the three emulsions might be altered. This effect is known as reciprocity failure: the reciprocal relationship between exposure and light intensity does not apply.

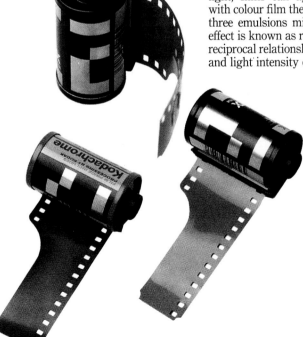

Each type of film is now identified by a bar code system known as DX coding. Modern electronic cameras can recognize these codes and from them register the speed of the film and number of exposures on the LCD panel.

Times of day

Dawn

Morning

Midday

Sunrise

The quality of daylight varies tremendously in different parts of the world and at different times of the year, depending on the angle of the sun in the sky. Just after the sun rises and immediately before it sets are the magic moments which can make the most mundane subjects worth photographing.

Dawn has wonderful photographic properties. The light is clean, clear and cold. Many car advertising pictures are shot at this time as the modelling effect of the light is so good. It is shadowless with little difference between the highlights and shadows. It is well worth getting up for this time of day—many of the best pictures are taken at dawn when most people are still in bed.

Sunrise brings a warm, romantic light containing more red than blue tones. The sun's rays are sharper than at sunset. There is high definition on directly lit subjects, but as the sun rises in the sky the quality of light changes quickly, leaving very little time to shoot.

Afternoon

Sunsets can never be chased so a prior knowledge of where the sun is going to drop is vital. Meter readings should be taken from one side of the sun and exposures should be bracketed. On automatic cameras matrix metering works well for sunset pictures. The computerized metering system can recognize a sunset and expose for the whole picture, not just the bright sun.

Dusk. After the sun has set the glow which remains provides a similar light to pre-dawn, but softer and full of colour. As the light level decreases, longer exposures are necessary. The indirect light softens hard surfaces.

Sunset

Morning. The fine light that lasts until about ten o'clock is popular with professional photographers when shooting fashion or travel assignments on location. The sun climbing in a blue sky provides a clean, almost colourless light. Visibility is good and shadows are clearly defined although not yet totally black.

Midday is not the best time for general photography since the sun is too directly overhead. There is a tremendous difference in exposure between shadows and highlight areas. The light is usually too hazy for landscape shots, although in the winter or after rain it can be suitable. In portraiture, eye sockets tend to fill in with hard shadows. This hard light with its black shadow areas can be used to advantage with a polarizing filter.

Afternoon. As the sun gets lower in the sky, modelling comes back into the landscape and the warm quality of the light is good for skin tones. This diffused light is best for backlighting. Water sparkles and the long shadows are blue.

Dusk

49

Daylight

God's light is best: daylight is the raw material of photography and has an infinite range of effects of which the serious photographer must be aware.

One of the old laws of photography was that the sun should always be on the photographer's back, but this no longer applies. With modern lenses pictures can be taken irrespective of the position of the sun. Light from a window enables good interior shots to be taken without flash if the subject is positioned with care, *right*.

With backlighting there is little detail other than in the subject, *below*. For portraits, readings must be taken off the subject's nose. Avoid a silhouette effect by exposing for the darkest part of the picture.

Shade is flattering to people because it is diffused, shadowless and flat. At midday, when direct light is too harsh, shade can be used to good effect, *below right*. Be careful when using colour film: shade can lend a blue or greenish cast.

Light is immovable. The position of the subject of the picture, and the angle of the camera to it, must be adjusted in relation to the light source. Give liberal exposure when using negative film in daylight. Never overexpose transparency film.

For a dramatic silhouette effect, expose for the highlights, allowing the subject to become just a shape. On automatic cameras use the manual override and set the exposure yourself—the automatic metering system will expose for the whole picture, not just the highlights.

In the morning or afternoon, a halo effect can be achieved by placing the subject between the sun and camera. If indoors, the window should be above and behind. Depending on the strength of the halo light required, a reflector may be used to fill the front of the subject with light. The background can be dark or it can be allowed to flare out completely. This is a flattering light.

51

Weather

Bad weather has as dramatic an effect on the quality of light as the changing angle of the sun. Don't be afraid of the wet or cold. Prepare the camera properly and shoot in conditions from which most people shelter.

Look after yourself, too. On a cold, wet day a warm anorak and good boots may contribute more to the success of a picture than a fancy lens.

Snow scenes like this Scottish landscape, *above*, have a blue cast which can be corrected with 81 series filters. Snow reflects light so be careful with exposures.

Fog gives muted colours, allowing key images to be picked out from the background, as in this London park scene, *left*. Bracket exposures to be sure of obtaining the picture you want in difficult conditions.

Rain makes surfaces glossy and highlights sparkle. This shot, *left*, was taken in Sri Lanka during the monsoon season.

After rain the clearing sky provides a clean, soft light as if the air has been washed, as in this shot of London's old Covent Garden market, *above*.

Gaps in storm clouds let through bursts of strong light. In this picture, *left*, taken in the Cotswolds, England, drama is increased by exposing for the highlights on the house at just the right moment, so making the sky seem even darker and stormier than it was.

Long exposure by moonlight can produce colour changes such as the purple cast on this Zanzibar mosque, *above*. On exposures over 30 seconds, movement of the moon will also be registered. Some film is not designed for long exposure use, so check before you try such a shot.

After sunset, daylight or tungsten transparency film can be used when photographing artificially lit subjects. Tungsten film gave the correct colour of this floodlit Portuguese cathedral, *left*.

53

Filters ☐ black and white

The use of filters can be divided into three categories: black and white filtration; colour compensation filters; and special effects (see pp.184–195). Each involves different principles, but the use of filters is simple once the basic ways in which they work are understood.

When using filters for black and white photography there is just one basic principle to understand. Filters lighten their own colour (and those in that area of the spectrum) and darken the complementary (opposite) colour.

A yellow filter, for example, holds the tone in a blue sky, while giving separation from the clouds. An orange filter darkens the sky, and red has a spectacular effect on the blue, turning it almost black in contrast to bright white clouds. Any element of red in the picture would lighten with each filter.

Take care with exposure when using filters with black and white film—they can increase the contrast in the negative.

Remember to expose for the shadows (especially in landscapes) otherwise the picture will include only highlight detail, with none in the shadows.

Professional photographers often use filters with black and white film to increase the tonal separation of pictures for press reproduction. For example, in a photograph of an orange car against a background of blue sea, the tone of the car and the sea would appear too similar in black and white for the car to stand out sufficiently. If a yellow filter is used, however, the car would be lightened and the sea darkened without any loss of detail.

In black and white portraiture the use of an orange filter can improve the appearance of spotty skin by lightening the tone of the spots. For smooth white skin tones, use red filters.

Polarizing filters are used to control reflections and also as neutral density filters in black and white photography.

Filters for use with black and white films in daylight

Subject	Effect	Filter
Blue sky	Natural	No 8 Yellow
	Darkened	No 15 Orange
	Dark	No 25 Red
	Almost black	No 29 Deep Red
	Day for night	No 25 Red plus Polarizing
Seascape with blue sky	Natural	No 8 Yellow
	Dark water	No 15 Orange
Sunsets	Natural	No 8 Yellow or none
	Increased contrast	No 15 Orange or No 25 Red
Distant landscapes	Natural	No 8 Yellow
	Haze reduction	No 15 Orange
	Greater reduction of haze	No 25 Red or No 29 Deep Red
Dominant foliage	Natural	No 8 Yellow or No 11 Yellow-Green
	Light	No 58 Green
Outdoor portraiture Sky background	Natural	No 11 Yellow-Green No 8 Yellow or Polarizing No 25 Red
Flowers and foliage	Natural	No 8 Yellow or No 11 Yellow-Green
Red and orange colours	Lighten for greater detail	No 25 Red
Dark blue and purple colours	Lighten for greater detail	None or No 47 Blue
Foliage	Lighten for greater detail	No 58 Green
Stone, wood, sand, snow etc, in sunlight, blue sky	Natural	No 8 Yellow
	Increased texture	No 15 Orange or No 25 Red

A 15 Orange filter gives increased contrast, separating areas of similar tone in the sky and the water. It is more effective than the yellow types sold to non-professionals as "cloud filters".

A 25 Red can be used in portraiture to make skin tones smooth and white. Backgrounds are also darkened, giving prominence to the subject.

The most dramatic filter for use with black and white film is the 29 Red, which turns the sky almost black while keeping the clouds white. As the blue is filtered out, the effect of haze is also reduced.

55

Filters □ colour

Colour compensating filters are used to change the colour temperature of the light falling on the subject. They can only be used with colour transparency film. If possible buy glass filters which are the best optical quality.

Compensating filters increase their own colour in the picture by filtering out the complementary colours. When shooting a portrait under a tree, for example, skin tones take on an unpleasant green cast from the leaves. By using a 10 Magenta (the complementary colour to green) the skin tone is brought back to normal without upsetting the greens of the background.

When skin tones are particularly important, as when shooting colour portraits, beauty, glamour or nude shots, they can be enhanced by use of the 81 series filters. These add warmth to skin tones, giving a richer, suntanned appearance. Care should be taken when shooting on Fuji film, which is browner in tone than the E6 process Ektachrome films. The 81 series are useful on dull, overcast days as they increase the saturation of all colours in the shot.

Also useful as "cosmetics" filters are the 1A and 2A—like the 81 they warm and intensify colours, but with a pink hue rather than the brownish tint of the 81 series.

Other filters correct the colour temperature of light to match the film being used. An 80B is used to balance daylight film for use in tungsten light. An 85B enables tungsten film to be used in daylight. (See also p.59 for the use of filtration when working with fluorescent and mixed light sources.)

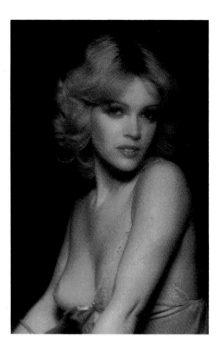

Polarizing filters

The polarizing filters are essential equipment for the serious colour photographer. They reduce polarized light and are used to hold saturation in directly lit subjects; for controlling reflective surfaces such as painted metal, glass and water; and for penetrating the reflections on transparent materials. These filters act in the same way as Polaroid sunglasses—which can be used over the lens if there is no filter available.

Polarizing filters are most often used to bring out the blue sky and cloud effects—the job done by red filters with black and white film. They also hold highlight detail and reproduce saturated "hard edge" colours on the beach, in sunny snow scenes or anywhere there is a lot of light bouncing around. When used with Kodachrome 25 and exposures made for the highlights, the shadows will drop out to black, creating a simple graphic effect. They are not effective on backlit subjects, sunsets or sunrises. Polarizing filters are adjustable and when there is a chance of obtaining a good shot, take several frames, each with a different degree of polarization.

UV (ultraviolet) and L39 filters, much used in the past, have virtually no effect on modern coated lenses. However, it is still advisable to use them since they help protect the lens.

By using an 81EF filter for the portrait, *left*, the skin tones are warmed and enhanced. A Softar filter softens the overall effect. To cut out unpleasant green cast on the skin from the trees, *above*, a 10 Magenta was used. Two uses of polarizing filters are illustrated. Reflections are cut out, *above right*, with the effect of seeing through the water. The sky in the picture, *right*, is made more dramatic—clouds are whitened and the blue made darker.

Magenta (M)	Green (G)	Cyan (C)	Red (R)	Yellow (Y)	Blue (B)
Absorbs green	Absorbs blue and red	Absorbs red	Absorbs blue and green	Absorbs blue	Absorbs red and green

Colour filtration with fluorescent light

Film type	Type of fluorescent lamp (written on tube)*					
	Daylight	White	Warm white	Warm white Deluxe	Cool white	Cool white Deluxe
Daylight	40M + 30Y +1 stop	20C + 30M +1 stop	40C + 40M +1⅓ stop	60C + 30M +1⅔ stop	30M +⅔ stop	30C + 20M +1 stop
Tungsten and Type L	85B + 30M +10Y +1⅔ stop	40M + 40Y + 1 stop	30M + 20Y + 1 stop	10Y +⅓ stop	50M + 60Y +1⅓ stop	10M + 30Y +⅔ stop
Type A	85B + 30M +10Y +1⅔ stop	40M + 30Y +1 stop	30M + 10Y +1 stop	None	50M + 50Y +1⅓ stop	10M + 20Y +⅔ stop
*Beware—colour balance alters with age						

Colour compensating filters are essential when shooting in fluorescent light or everything will turn out green. If you do not have a colour temperature meter use the chart above as a rough guide to which filters to use and by how much to increase exposure. (See also p.59.)

Compact flash units □ 1

Before introducing a new light source, consider whether use of a tripod and long exposure might better retain the mood of the photograph. A particular effect of light can often be the stimulus for a picture. But that effect can easily be lost by using additional lighting. Many photographers automatically turn to flash because the subject is too dark to shoot with a hand held camera.

But when additional lighting really is necessary, the latest technology takes the uncertainty out of flash photography. TTL flash metering is particularly effective when flash is used in conjunction with daylight. A sensor in the camera measures the amount of light reflected on the film surface and determines the flash output, taking account of the existing light.

Even in darkness, built-in illuminators on some electronic flash units allow autofocus cameras to function perfectly. Below certain light levels the illuminator automatically turns on to allow the autofocus to operate.

Electronic flash units also offer features such as adjustable heads so that the angle of flash can be varied.

Nikon Speedlight SB-24

Vivitar 283

Sunpak

Metz 45CT-4

The Nikon Speedlight SB-24, a powerful electronic flash unit, offers automatic TTL flash output control with the F4 and F-801 and automatic exposure control with any Nikon SLR camera. The built-in autofocus illuminator comes into operation in low light conditions and allows correctly focused pictures to be taken even in darkness. The SB-24 also has an adjustable head which can be tilted down to −7° or up to 90°, or rotated 90° clockwise and 180° counter-clockwise. All information relevant to the exposure is displayed on an LCD panel. The Speedlight is powered by ordinary penlight batteries.

The Metz 45CT-4 has long been the press photographer's flash because it has a fast recycle time when set on automatic. It is powered by either rechargeable nickel cadmium or ordinary batteries.

The Sunpak is a cheap but reliable two battery unit. It is powerful at close range, but falls off rapidly and is often used as second "fill" light.

The Vivitar 283 is a dedicated flash unit that fits all camera systems. The head can be tilted for bounced flash and includes filters. The Vivitar is one of the most versatile flash units and, when used with an extension lead, can provide a variety of effects.

Mixed light sources

Taking pictures with colour film under mixed light conditions can be a problem even for the most experienced photographers. Colour temperature meters are useful but expensive; you can manage with a normal meter.

When faced with daylight, tungsten and fluorescent light in the same shot, be methodical. Use a hand meter to find out which is the dominant light source. Turn out the artificial light and meter the daylight. Then turn on the tungsten, measure that and do the same with the fluorescent. If the daylight is the dominant light source, choose daylight film. (Any tungsten light will only warm the colour; 400 ISO film copes well with this combination.)

Ignore the fluorescent light if its influence is slight—the warmth of the tungsten light will help to balance it. If the fluorescent is substantial, balance it out with a 10 Magenta filter on the camera.

If tungsten is the dominant light source, choose a tungsten film. The daylight will then produce a blue cast and the fluorescent a green cast, depending on how much of each is present. Remember that colour is usually preferred warm rather than cold and it can be warmed up with 10 Magenta and 81B filters.

If fluorescent is the dominant light source, consult the table on p.57 as a guide. Fluorescent makes a good light for black and white, but it can produce a disastrous colour balance if the photographer is not aware of the type of tube he is shooting under—each produces a different colour balance.

When shooting a foreground figure in a large fluorescent-lit room a 30 Magenta filter on the camera will correct the light. Although the room will now be correctly colour balanced the foreground will be magenta. To overcome this problem take an exposure reading of the room—for example, 1/15 second at f8 (64 ISO)—and then light the foreground figure with the flash filtered by a 30 Green and balanced at f8. This brings the figure back to normal while the room remains corrected.

Fluorescent lights are most often encountered in buildings with high ceilings, such as factories, where identifying the type of tube may be difficult. To find out what tubes are fitted to the lights, ask the janitor or whoever orders the replacements. Large sheets of fluorescent correcting gelatine, made for the movie industry, can be stuck over the tubes to balance the light to daylight. If it is too difficult to correct the balance, use colour negative film which allows more opportunity for adjustment at print stage.

Compact flash units □ 2

A naturalist and his pet owl were photographed at sunset using the latest flash technology—matrix programmable flash balanced to the natural light. The flash was off the camera, but connected by a speedlight cord. An infrared beam from the flash head calculated both the amount of flash needed to light the man and a suitable aperture and relayed this information to the camera. The flash was fired just as the owl landed on the man's hand.

The fish market, *below*, was lit by dedicated manual flash balanced to the ambient light. A reading of the level of background light was taken first and the flash set to give a similar reading. The picture was shot at 1/15 second to allow the natural light to register. Because there was too much movement for such a long exposure, use of flash was essential to freeze the action as well as to light the subjects in the foreground of the picture.

Two compact flashes—one mounted on the camera hot shoe and the other positioned in the background—were used to light this elegant reconstructed drawing room at the Burrell Museum, Glasgow, *above*. The two were balanced to make the foreground and background light the same. While the camera flash brought out the detail in the foreground chair the second flash was necessary to illuminate the rest of the room.

Red eye occurs when flash is directly in line with the eyes—light is reflected off them and causes a red glow, *below*. To avoid red eye ask the subject to look up at the flash rather than positioning him in line with it. Alternatively, diffuse the flash or bounce it off the wall.

Intricate carving on this wall of a Buddhist temple, *below left*, required a strong direct flash to pick up the detail.

Using compact flash

Compact flash units are often used when photographing people. They give reliable exposures on normal lenses, but all have their idiosyncrasies. Shoot several rolls of film to discover how your unit works.

Vary the position of the flash and its angle in relation to the subject to produce different effects.

Further tests can be made to find out how filters affect exposure.

Two compact flashes lit this portrait of the head chef of the Drake Hotel, Chicago, but with a shutter speed of 25 seconds so that the candlelight also registered. A more natural look is often achieved by using a slower than indicated shutter speed, allowing ambient light to register, in conjunction with flash.

Painting with light is a creative flash technique. The first picture, *below left*, was taken with a 20 second exposure, using only the natural light in the church. It is too dark, and reveals little detail. For the second picture, *below right*, the camera was on open shutter with a black card held over the lens. An assistant walked around the church, keeping the same distance from the walls, and fired a series of 15 flashes. With each flash the photographer removed the card to allow light to reach the film. The process took several minutes, but the shutter was only open for about 15 seconds.

Hold flash at arm's length above camera on extension cable. More modelling, less contrast makes this a flattering light. No "red eye" with colour.

Flash at 45° from camera, held about 30cm (12in) above height of model. Use another lamp to test positioning of flash. Nose shadow should join with cheek shadow.

Flash at 90° to the model about 30cm (12in) in front at face height. Be careful not to fill in the eye shadow. Again, check with another light source.

Flash held 30–60cm (12–24in) above model, aimed directly at her face. Subject should look upward to achieve flattering chin line.

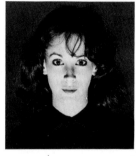

Flash aimed from the feet of the photographer. This gives a spooky effect and is not a flattering light.

Flash bounced off a side wall. A soft, flattering light. Electric eye picks up off subject. Overexpose one stop to give shadow detail with black and white film.

Top bounce is soft light but can make bags under eyes prominent. Overexpose one stop to minimize bags.

Flash behind the head against a dark background such as a curtain. Overexpose three stops. Use reflector to fill face.

Silhouette. Flash is directly behind the model, aimed at wall. Level of exposure governs whiteness of wall. Overexpose at least one stop.

Lighting □ 1

Creatively used, lighting can bring atmosphere and meaning to a photograph. This picture of a hospital CAT scan (Computerized Axial Tomography) department was intended to show that the most up-to-date technology was in use—but in caring hands. The hard, clinical atmosphere of the equipment had to be tempered by human warmth.

There were several problems. The photographer had no control over the room; everything had to remain where it was and be worked round. It was important that the information on the television screens registered so the shot had to be taken in the dark with a long exposure of about 20 seconds. Also, because the nurse was close to the camera and the patient farther away, a small aperture, f22, was selected to hold the picture sharp from foreground to background.

The job of the lighting was to create an atmosphere while featuring the main elements in the picture. Four lights were used; their positions are shown in the diagram.

The light from the spot on the nurse also gave a reading of f22. This spot was positioned so that no light fell onto the

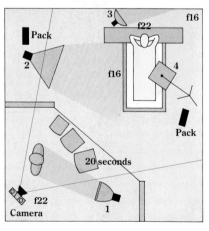

Lights used were (1) spotlight with hood and directional grille; (2) 1m (3.3ft) soft box; (3) 138cm (15in) soft dish; (4) metal box light with grille.

screens but there was good modelling light on her face. Great care had to be taken that no reflection showed in the glass screen between control room and scanner.

The final picture was shot in the dark, lit by flashlight, with an exposure of 20 seconds at f22 on Kodachrome 64.

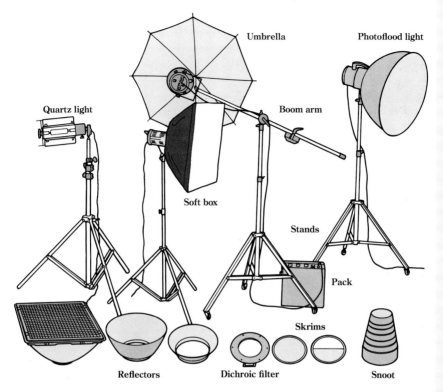

Umbrella

Photoflood light

Quartz light

Boom arm

Soft box

Stands

Pack

Skrims

Reflectors   Dichroic filter   Snoot

Bowen's and Elincrom equipment is used here to illustrate the range of lighting now available.

The soft box attachment is self-contained. All the power selection, sync, slave and model light controls are in the head, which plugs straight into the mains supply. It has enough power for general 35mm photography but it is generally better to use two heads to light a picture. Box lights range in size from 0.5m (1.5ft) to 6m (20ft) square.

Quartz or tungsten can be used instead of flash, the only difference being that the speed of flash light makes the resulting picture sharper.

Quartz lights are mainly used in the film industry. The portable kits on the market are useful as secondary lights, in conjunction with flash, for industrial and location photography.

Photoflood tungsten lights are still favoured by many photographers who consider the softness of their light to be ideal for portraiture. For all lights make sure stands are strong.

Striplights are special studio lights. They require a lot of power and are generally used with large format cameras for lighting backgrounds.

The pack can run up to four heads of various types. All the controls for the lights are on the pack. Several packs can be linked together to power one big light. Keep packs off wet surfaces and concrete.

Umbrellas are used to soften and spread light. The gold version gives the light a warming cast (equivalent to an 81B filter), which is ideal for skin tones.

Reflectors and snoots control the spread of light and are available in various shapes and sizes. Use dichroic filters on quartz lights to correct to daylight and skrims to soften the light.

Lighting □ 2

Two types of artificial light are available to the photographer: tungsten and electronic flash.

Tungsten lamps, which remain on all the time, allow you to see what effects are being created. When shooting in colour, artificial (type B) film must be used. Quartz bulbs are in the same colour temperature range as tungsten bulbs, although they are much brighter. Even so, many lamps and a long exposure are needed to simulate the effect of flash. Quartz lamps are good to use when many different sources of illumination are needed since they give localized, controllable light.

Electronic flash runs off domestic power or generators and provides a light balanced to within the range of daylight (5400–5600 Kelvin). In its naked state it is a hard, clear and intense light. Professional photographers use such high wattage flash to achieve maximum picture quality.

The larger the area of a light source the better the quality of the light—bounce it back off an umbrella or flat reflector or use a diffuser.

Attachments are available which fit over the flash and diffuse the light or try taping tissue or tracing paper over it for a soft effect.

Well diffused light comes closest to the "north light" preferred by painters. Remember that the closer the light source is to the subject, the softer its effect.

Use a single direct light source to pick out the features of the face, *above left*. Keep the light higher than the head and don't let the eye sockets fill in. This light emphasizes the eyes and moulding of the face. The same set-up, *above right*, but the light is reflected off a white surface, softening the features but retaining the roundness of the face.

The lighting of old Hollywood black and white films inspired this lighting set-up, used for both pictures, *above*. Their film was so slow they had to light everywhere. Having created a set-up, walk around to see the effect of the light from other angles. Here, the model is lit from back and front; the spot at the back holds him off the background.

This complicated set-up is good for full-length fashion shots. Textures stand out well. The angle of camera to model determines how much light is on the model.

A spotlight creates a theatrical mood, emphasizing the cheek bones and narrowing the face; flattering for a rounded or fat face. But use with care—it is too harsh for bad skin.

A soft lighting set-up, *below,* is ideal for a still life of rounded objects and a flattering light for nudes. Often used for mother and child pictures on baby goods packs.

Beauty lighting, *below.* Black reflectors, close to the model's face, hollow the cheeks. The model should look up a little so the face is evenly lit. Good with a soft focus filter.

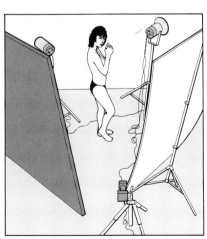

Backgrounds

Good photography requires the rigorous searching out not only of the beautiful but also of the ugly. What separates the good photographer from the casual snapshooter is the ability to eliminate ugliness from the backgrounds of pictures.

Be on the lookout for things such as lampposts which appear to grow out of the heads of subjects, and change position to avoid them. Get into the habit of using the preview button on your camera: what is unnoticeable when the lens is wide open may appear terribly distracting when the lens is stopped down.

On location
When shooting portraits outdoors a wide open aperture keeps the background out of focus. This is especially effective when using long lenses where the depth of field is naturally limited. Mirror lenses produce their own distinctive doughnut shapes on highlights in out-of-focus backgrounds.

Choose plain, simple textures for backgrounds which enhance the subject. Sand, water, pebbles and brick walls make good neutral backgrounds.

Sky is a good background for some shots, but be careful with the exposure readings at close range, otherwise the pictures will be underexposed. A white sheet hung on a clothes line makes a fine background when backlit. A white reflector should then be used to reflect light back onto the subject. When shooting colour portraits a gold reflector gives more pleasing skin tones.

Interiors
To make a large, continuous background area with no floor edge, professionals use Colorama paper. This comes in large rolls, 1.3m (4.6ft) to 3.6m (12ft) wide by 12,

To obtain the half lit, half in shadow effect, *above,* a single well diffused light source is used. It lights the right side of the face but is masked from the right side background by a screen.

On the left side a white reflector bounces light onto the background but not onto the left side of the face. By experimenting with the angles of screen and reflector, and framing the subject tightly, the degree of contrast can be altered.

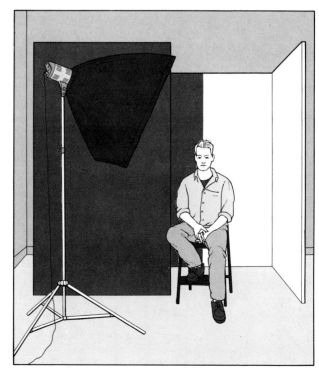

25 or 50m (40, 80, 165ft) in length, and is available in an enormous range of colours.

Black velvet absorbs light and is an excellent solid background when photographing front-lit still life or people, especially for stroboscopic multiple image pictures. The velvet should be thick and of good quality. A transparency light box makes a good "white-out" backlit background for small, still-life subjects. Place reflectors all around the object for a beautiful rounded light.

Pressure pack (aerosol) paint spray can be used to take the flatness out of plain-coloured backgrounds. Combinations of colour applied in short bursts blend together.

Projecting slides onto a screen or paper background and then lighting the foreground subject can be effective.

A good continuous background for still life is plastic laminate, which can be bent into a curve. It can also be wiped dry—especially useful when shooting liquids or food, which could spill and demand a new set-up each time the paper got wet. Large rolls of white plastic are available for this type of use. Opaque acrylic makes a fine background material for obtaining a flat bottom light.

Some photographers make large out-of-focus prints of scenes, in front of which they pose their models. This can give the effect of an outdoor location in the studio. Projection screens can be used effectively as portrait backgrounds, as can large black or white blinds.

Collect beautiful things, such as pieces of wood, marble or glass, to use when the right subject appears. These can add an extra dimension to still-life shots. Slate, and even high-tech steel mesh, can add interesting texture to backgrounds.

The studio background, *right,* is spray-painted paper. The diagram, *below,* shows how it is possible to have one set-up with either an overall light or a dark background. A heavily diffused single light above the subject gives an overall light on both bear and background. By taking the background farther back the subject sits in a pool of light against black. Plenty of light is bounced into the shadows.

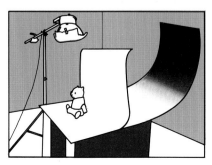

Tripods □ 1

A tripod is an indispensable part of a photographer's kit. It must be portable—although the ideal tripod would be so heavy as to be immovable—but the lightest tripods are too flimsy to be of any use. Extended legs should not flex under pressure, nor should leg locks be able to slip. If the head wobbles when a camera is mounted the tripod is useless. Test thoroughly for any movement with the longest and heaviest lens available.

Tripods are essential when shooting with long focal length lenses, which are impossible to hold securely by hand.

They are also needed to prevent camera shake when using slow shutter speeds.

As a rough guide, use a tripod when shooting with a 500mm lens at less than 1/500 second; or with a 200mm lens at less than 1/200 second.

Even when it is possible to hand hold the camera, a tripod allows for extra precision and control in composition. The photographer can leave the camera in position while making any final adjustments to the shot.

The best tripods have a central column, which is reversible and adjustable in

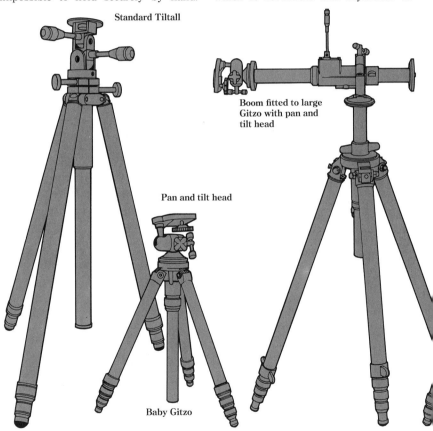

Standard Tiltall

Boom fitted to large Gitzo with pan and tilt head

Pan and tilt head

Baby Gitzo

Standard size tripods, such as the Tiltall, Gitzo or Linhof, are for studio or location use, although they are too heavy to be carried around all day by one person with a bag full of equipment. They extend to a height of 2.1m (7ft) and can be fitted with a boom.

The central column can be reversed to hold the camera close to the ground.

The Baby Gitzo is an outstanding portable tripod which can be extended to eye level. With the ball and socket head removed it fits easily into a suitcase or height, for low-level shooting. They also have heads which pan and tilt so that the precise position and angle of the camera can be adjusted. The bottoms of the legs are fitted with rubber caps for general use, but these can be removed to expose spikes for sticking into soft ground. When working on surfaces such as sand fit "snow shoe" adaptors to the feet.

The best tripod for the 35mm photographer is one that can be packed into a suitcase. It should be strong as well as compact with both low-angle and eye-level capability.

Spirit levels are essential when the picture has to be perfectly square—for example, when shooting architecture, paintings or documents. They are also useful in close-up work when it is hard to square up the picture, and to get horizons flat when framing with a wide angle lens. Some tripods have built-in spirit levels, but there are separate units available which fit into the camera hot shoe, *below right.*

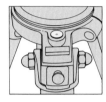

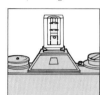

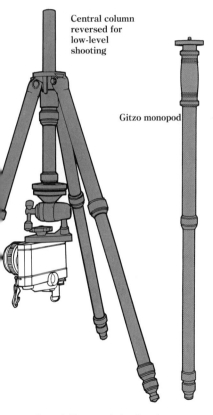

Central column reversed for low-level shooting

Gitzo monopod

Leitz tabletop tripod

The Leitz tabletop unit is a miniature tripod, with ball and socket head. Although small enough to be used almost anywhere it is extremely solid, more so than some larger stands. When folded, it is less than 30cm (1ft) in length.

can be carried between the handles of a camera case.

Monopods are lighter to carry and useful in crowds and confined spaces where tripod legs would get in the way of other people. They are popular with news and sport photographers.

When shooting without a tripod, use a tabletop stand to steady the camera against any available surface. If there is no wall or table close to hand the camera can be braced against the photographer's chest.

Tripods ☐ 2

There are many occasions when a photographer needs to be mobile and can only carry a small tripod. If clamps or rests of some kind are also carried the camera can be kept rigid in any situation.

Even when a camera is mounted on a tripod or a clamp and slow shutter speeds are being used, it is still advisable to lock the mirror up—the mirror return action can cause the camera to shake and ruin the picture.

When more than one camera is used to take shots of the same subject, clamps enable one tripod to hold several bodies. Use this method, *right*, for a non-repeatable shot, or if the action is moving toward the camera.

Clamps can be used to place cameras in

Bean bags provide a solid base for a camera, *below*. They can be useful for low-level shooting, or when a ledge such as a car window is being used as a rest. A soft camera bag can also be employed in the same way.

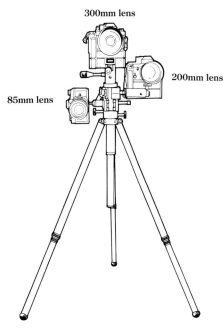

300mm lens

200mm lens

85mm lens

A monopod is suited to situations when a tripod would prove too bulky or slow to use. By bracing it against his body, *below*, the photographer becomes a part of the stand, his two legs and the monopod making an effective tripod. When kneeling or sitting the knee provides additional support. Slipping the right arm through the neck strap provides extra rigidity.

inaccessible corners. If fixed to solid objects they can even be preferable to a tripod. With a small ball and socket camera mount, most types of lighting or woodwork clamps can be adapted to hold a camera. The tripod screw thread on most cameras is a 6mm ($\frac{1}{4}$in) Whitworth.

Clamps can be attached to most objects, and, by using glazier's vacuum suckers, they can even be mounted onto plate glass windows. They must be strong, however. Be wary of anything with plastic tightening screws which may break under stress.

Use of clamps can allow a photographer to get shots which would otherwise be impossible. A camera attached to an expanding pole, for example, can be placed high up in the corner of a room. If the presence of the photographer is likely to be disruptive, cameras can be positioned prior to shooting and operated by cable release or electronic remote controls.

With remote releases, autowinds and automatic exposure control, clamps open up opportunities for picture taking. Such methods do, however, require careful setting up and an exact knowledge of the desired shot.

Spring grip clamp fixed to a plank of wood.

Stanley strap clamp fixed to a tree trunk.

A C-clamp attached to the top of a ladder.

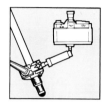

A C-clamp screwed to a tripod leg.

A lighting boom with camera mounting attachment and a long cable release, *below*, can be used to set up shots from positions from which the photographer cannot reach. It makes a useful arrangement when attempting to shoot out of windows or from the corners of high-ceilinged rooms.

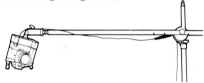

A pistol grip holds a long lens steady at slower shutter speeds. Bracing yourself against a wall further increases stability.

When using a tripod in high wind try joining two camera straps together to make a foot hold on which to exert downward pressure, *below*.

A bag of heavy stones hung from the tripod head, *below*, also adds stability.

Cases

The job of a camera bag is to protect expensive equipment, so get the best you can afford. A soft bag with plenty of compartments is probably the best for general use, but metal cases provide better protection.

Pack the bag carefully so you know where each piece of equipment is—it may be needed in a hurry. Never pack the bag too full—carrying a heavy load all day uses a lot of energy. Try putting at least some equipment about the person or in pockets.

Inflatable air bags give good protection to contents and fold up to pocket size when deflated. They come in a variety of sizes, including individual lens bags. They are especially useful during rough car or boat trips when luggage can get thrown around.

Chamois leather can be made into pouches or used loose to protect equipment. It insulates and can be used to clean lenses. Lens pouches are vital to keep metal from rubbing against metal. Buy the best—the felt lining on cheap pouches can come off and clog the camera.

Soft bags such as the Lowe Pro hold lots of equipment with easy access and,

For the photographer on the move, skiing or trekking, there are two types of bag that leave the hands free: the day pack with built-in camera case, worn on the back, and the ski belt bag, worn around the waist.

when packed carefully, protect equipment well. Top and bottom should be waterproof. When carried over the shoulder, soft bags leave the hands free.

Hard leather tubes are the best lens cases to use with a soft camera bag. They can also be used to carry a selection of filters screwed together.

Lead-lined travellers' bags offer some protection from X-rays, but security

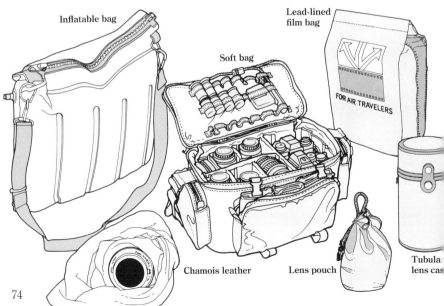

Inflatable bag

Soft bag

Lead-lined film bag

FOR AIR TRAVELERS

Chamois leather

Lens pouch

Tubula lens cas

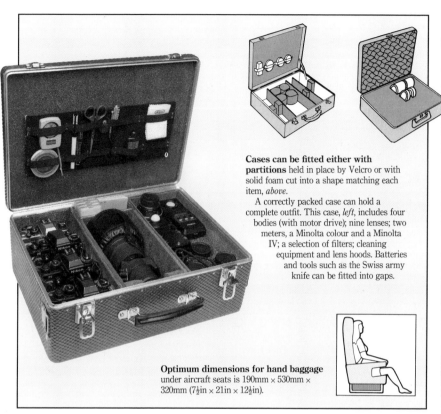

Cases can be fitted either with partitions held in place by Velcro or with solid foam cut into a shape matching each item, *above*.

A correctly packed case can hold a complete outfit. This case, *left*, includes four bodies (with motor drive); nine lenses; two meters, a Minolta colour and a Minolta IV; a selection of filters; cleaning equipment and lens hoods. Batteries and tools such as the Swiss army knife can be fitted into gaps.

Optimum dimensions for hand baggage under aircraft seats is 190mm × 530mm × 320mm (7½in × 21in × 12½in).

Insulated Kodak bag

Ever-ready case

Fisherman's pouches

crews often turn up the power of machines until they can see what is inside. Carry film on the person.

Metal cases provide good protection in all weathers. Rox and Halliburton are the best makes. Silver cases reflect the sun, while black ones absorb heat.

The Kodak insulated bag is primarily for carrying film but is also useful for storing cameras in hot cars or on the beach. Use freezer sachets to keep the temperature low.

Fisherman's pouches can be used to carry small items such as filters and are cheaper than photographic pouches. Ever-ready cases are available in soft or hard versions and do provide protection, especially if no other type of case or bag is used. Their size precludes use with telephoto lenses.

Viewers and screens

The waist-level finder provides a direct view of the uncorrected image on the ground glass screen. It is possible to draw on the screen for composition reference. A four-sided hood aids focusing by shielding the screen from unwanted light. This viewer is useful when the camera cannot be brought to the eye, for shooting from low down or from overhead.

The action finder is a magnifying reflex viewer which enables the photographer to see the entire image with his eye some way from the lens. It is useful for shooting fast-moving subjects such as sport or wildlife, when the action must be followed with both eyes. The large eyepiece makes it suitable for use when spectacles or goggles are worn.

The pentaprism head through which the image is viewed is a feature of all SLR cameras. Its optically precise prism corrects the image which has been reversed by the lens.

For certain applications, where focusing is critical or difficult, photographers may prefer to use alternative viewers or ground glass focusing screens. The facility for changing these parts is only available on some sophisticated cameras.

On automatic cameras the electronic meter circuitry prevents the removal of the viewing heads. There are, however, adaptors to aid close focusing which can be attached to fixed head cameras.

Eyepiece correction lenses are available for wearers of spectacles to correct the magnification of prescription lenses. Rubber eye caps prevent stray light entering the viewfinder.

Eyepiece correction lens

Rubber eye cap

Focusing screens
Like viewing heads, focusing screens can be interchanged only on certain cameras. A choice of screens is available for both the Nikon F4 and F-801 (N8008) and these are easily changed. A comprehensive range is also available for sophisticated manual cameras.

The standard Nikon screen shows a split image in the centre of a plain screen, which is aligned when brought into focus. It is not suitable when a lens with a small aperture is fitted.

The B-type screen, *right*, is the standard and is supplied with both the F-801 and F4 cameras. A selection of other types is illustrated.

The 6x focusing finder magnifies the image on the screen and is useful in scientific or close-up photography. Its enlargement permits critical focusing of the whole image, while its complex optical construction allows adjustment to individual eyesight. As with all non-reflex viewers the uncorrected image on the screen is seen reversed, as in a mirror.

The right-angle finder is not a replacement but an accessory to the pentaprism. By swivelling the eyepiece the image can be viewed from above or from the sides. It is mainly used with a copying stand, but is also useful when the camera is in a tight corner. With the camera turned upright, pictures can be framed by looking straight down into the viewer.

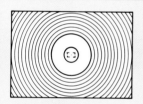

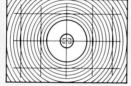

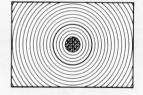

Type B: Matte/Fresnel field with two reference circles, 5mm and 12mm in diameter and autofocus brackets. The screen for general photography.

Type E: Matte/Fresnel field with 5mm and 12mm circles, autofocus brackets and etched horizontal and vertical lines. Ideal for architectural photography.

Type J: Matte/Fresnel field with central microprism focusing spot 5mm in diameter and a 12mm circle. Useful for general photography.

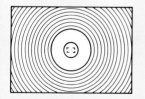

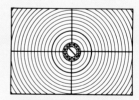

Type U: Matte/Fresnel field with reference circles 5mm and 12mm in diameter and autofocus brackets. Suitable for use with telephoto lenses longer than 200mm.

Type K: Matte/Fresnel field with 3mm split image spot surrounded by a microprism doughnut. Good for subjects with straight lines and ill-defined contours.

Type P: like K, but with a split image rangefinder line at a 45° angle and etched horizontal and vertical lines as an aid to composition.

Motor drives

Cable releases are used when making long exposures with camera on tripod, eliminating camera shake caused by human contact. Double releases work two cameras.

Soft release buttons are left permanently on camera by some photographers. The button is more accessible than the normal shutter button and the action easier on slow shutter speeds. The air release cable is 30m (98ft) long. It is used for single shots and can be fitted to any make of camera.

The long release is used with a motor drive. It plugs into the camera body and can be as long as the piece of cable. The plug can be removed and wired to a transmitter or underwater housing.

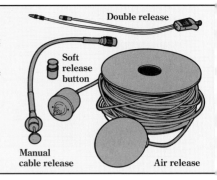

Double release

Soft release button

Manual cable release

Air release

An automatic winder transports the film and resets the shutter automatically. With this, several frames a second can be exposed.

A motor drive is a more sophisticated piece of equipment. It can shoot more frames per second, has a fast automatic rewind, unlike the smaller units, and allows multiple exposures to be made. Remote, radio controlled and data back equipment can also be fitted onto the unit.

Motor drives are popular for use in sport, news, surveillance and sequential photography. The single most important feature of motor drives is that the eye does not have to leave the viewfinder

when the camera is wound on. It can concentrate solely on the image in the finder. But remember, with fast action an image seen in the finder is a missed picture. The ability to anticipate the action has to be just as keen, whether or not a motor drive is being used.

Shooting indiscriminately at four frames a second is not a guarantee of getting the picture. Follow the action by eye rather than relying on shutter speeds of 1/2000 second to capture motion.

Motorized winders make it possible to bracket exposures incredibly quickly, but the new range of data backs will even bracket automatically.

The F4 operates in four modes on motor drive. It is capable of a single frame to 5.7 frames a second or one frame per second on silent mode. It can be set for continuous high or low shutter speed.

The MF-21 Multi-Control back for the Nikon F-801 is a useful extra which can imprint data such as time, date, frame number. It can also control various camera functions such as automatic bracketing.

A pistol grip with connection to motor drive is useful when using heavy lenses. There is also a connection to the camera for single shots.

Be careful when using pistol grips, especially when shooting action with a fast shutter. There is a lot of play from trigger to release button.

Long release

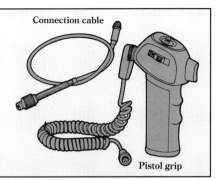

Connection cable

Pistol grip

Nikon MD4 motor drive with 250 exposure magazine. The film is bulk loaded. Cassettes can be unloaded in sections as they are shot.

The modulite remote control unit, *right,* is a receiver mounted on the camera and triggered by a hand unit emitting an infrared light beam. In a confined space the beam can be bounced off walls or around corners. Two cameras can be triggered using one control unit. This allows the photographer to shoot from three places at once and get a variety of angles on the subject.

A more sophisticated remote control is the radio transmitter/receiver set, which has a range of 0.7km (0.4mi). It can operate three cameras and is designed to be interference free at all times. It has many uses, wildlife, sport or news coverage, for example. The camera can be pre-positioned hours before an event, such as a state occasion, in a location that would be inaccessible during the event.

Accessories

Compass—well worth carrying to find out where the sun will be.

Filters. Of the many available, Cokin filters are made of solid gelatine and their range of more than 200 types includes special effects. Wratten filters are flimsy gelatine and come in a variety of types for black and white and colour correction use. They fit any holder and portable flash units. Glass filters are the best optical quality and there are many makes. Choose glass when only a limited range of filters is carried. Always use glass Polaroid filters—cheap ones turn deep blues greenish on E6 transparency film. Nikon's polarizing filter is the best.

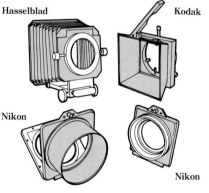

Hasselblad   Kodak

Nikon

Nikon

Filter holders. There are three basic types. Kodak make a cheap plastic holder which fits any lens and holds glass or gelatine filters. The Nikon type includes a built-in lens hood. Bellows holders, such as the Hasselblad or the cheaper Ambico models, hold filters on the front and rear of the unit and work on most lenses. They improve performance on long lenses as they cut out unwanted flare.

French flag is a black felt-covered piece of aluminium on a multi-jointed arm. Useful with wide aperture (or wide angle lenses) as it shades the light source from the lens.

Infrared flash trigger. This triggering system attached to the camera, with a receiver linked to a light, allows you to dispense with a flash sync lead. Useful when you want to put lights close to the subject and shoot on a long lens. The trigger has an effective range of about 50m (165ft).

Panorama tripod head allows the camera to be moved in fixed stages for making up composite prints from several different negatives.

Retort stands are useful for holding small reflectors or mirrors for use in still-life set-ups.

Rosco space blanket material is available in 1.8m × 1.2m (6ft × 4ft) sheets in silver/silver, silver/gold and silver/blue combinations. Often more useful than a hand flash, they kick back so much light that they may have to be held far back from the subject. Can also be used as a background. When folded they measure only 7cm × 5cm (3 × 5in).

Rubber eye caps help cut out light from behind the photographer's head which interferes with the image seen in the finder. Eyelashes often create shadows in the viewfinder.

Rubber lens hoods are more convenient than metal ones when shooting in crowded areas where cameras get jostled. A rigid (metal) hood increases the length of the lens, thereby putting more strain on the lens mount. Rubber types are washable, they do not get hot and don't scratch—scratches can cause flare. But don't use rubber hoods in a helicopter—they blow out of shape.

Silica gel absorbs moisture. Always keep a sachet in the bag with camera or film.

Spirit levels that fit directly onto the hot shoe are vital for any picture that requires a level camera.

Step ladder with two or three steps is invaluable for shooting over the heads of crowds or down onto a subject. Can also be used as a makeshift tripod, either with a clamp or by resting the camera on the top step.

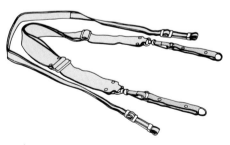

Straps. Use wide straps: they disperse the weight of the camera and lessen the strain on the shoulder from heavy motor drives or long lenses. Good straps have long lugs with dog collar fittings and

buckles each side which do not settle on the shoulder and dig into the neck. Rolled up, they can be used to fill out the corners of the camera bag. Nylon straps with non-slip padded shoulder pieces fix directly onto the camera and have no buckles to catch in the hair. They are good to use with lightweight equipment. Always buy good quality straps.

Three-way flash sync. Used to link three flash heads to the camera.

Tripod bush adaptor is used when camera thread and tripod screw do not match. Check the length of tripod screws, especially if using an adaptor. Screws that are too long can damage the internal workings of the camera.

Vacuum sucker sticks even to shiny surfaces and can hold a second flash unit when required. A magic eye on the vacuum sucker triggers this second flash when the first goes off.

Household objects

Photographers who are interested in making pictures as well as just taking them should have most of these household tools and objects close at hand. They can have many uses and sometimes a pair of pliers, spare plug or piece of tape is essential to the success of a photograph. A painting might need to be hung on a wall for atmosphere in a shot, a light might have to be taped up, or a candle used to aid focusing when shooting in the dark with compact flash. (The candle would not be needed with autofocus and TTL flash!)

Always be as well prepared as possible. With a comprehensive tool kit, the photographer is ready to make any repairs or adaptations that are needed.

The basic tools should include ratchet and electrical screwdrivers; multi-purpose screwdriver kit; wire strippers; long nose pliers (which can be filed down for use in tight areas); insulated heavy pliers; big scissors; retractable blade knife for heavy cutting and retractable blade scalpel for fine cutting jobs; coiled nylon/terylene mountaineering strap for securing cases and adding weights to tripod.

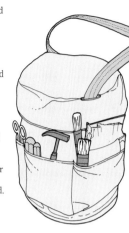

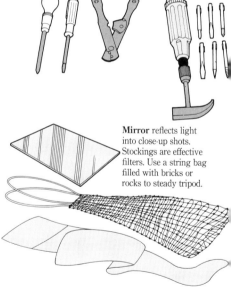

A jeweller's tool kit includes a variety of small screwdrivers. Essential for the minute screws on cameras and lenses, which tend to vibrate loose.

Battery flashlight, candle and pencil light. Always carry spare plugs, including an adaptable travel plug.

Mirror reflects light into close-up shots. Stockings are effective filters. Use a string bag filled with bricks or rocks to steady tripod.

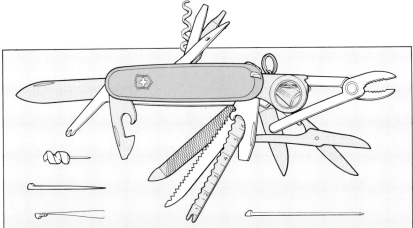

The Swiss army knife is as important as any photographic accessory and the latest models hold an amazing array of blades, screwdrivers, saws, scissors, pliers and so on. As well as doing the job they were designed for, blades have photographic applications: bottle opener can be used on stubborn cassettes; tweezers or toothpick for taking hair or fluff out of the camera.

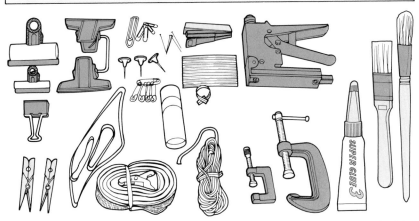

The biggest variety of clips, pegs, pins and clamps should be carried. There are always things to be held in place, from paper backgrounds to ill-fitting clothes. A powerful staple gun is a vital tool; string, superglue, rubber bands, drawing pins (thumbtacks) and paper clips are always handy. A selection of clamps hold heavier equipment and props. Hard and soft brushes are for cleaning equipment.

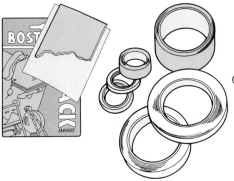

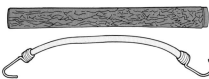

Aluminium foil can be used as a reflector and shaped to fit behind objects. Elasticated luggage strap is useful for securing bags. Blu-tack and a variety of tapes are needed for different applications. Strong and cloth backed, gaffer tape holds most things. Masking tape is used to stick paper. Plastic, clear adhesive and double-sided all have their uses.

Equipment chart □ I

It is possible to take most types of picture with one camera and one lens, but as a photographer's enthusiasm grows, so does the need for a versatile system. This chart is a guide to the equipment discussed so far, and its application to the most popular types of photography. The most useful equipment for handling a photographer's specific interest is listed against the subject heading.

CAMERA TYPES							
	Manual	Automatic	Nikonos	Widelux	Miniature	Autowind/motor drives	Fisheye
Portraits (studio)	📷	📷				📷	
Portraits (location)		📷					
Children		📷					
Weddings		📷				📷	
Photojournalism	📷	📷			📷	📷	
Out for the day		📷			📷		
Still life (studio)	📷	📷					
Still life (location)	📷	📷					
Close-up	📷	📷					
Close-up wildlife	📷	📷				📷	
Sport	📷	📷				📷	
Landscape	📷	📷		📷			
Aerial		📷				📷	
Marine		📷	📷				
Beauty	📷	📷					
Nude (studio)	📷	📷					
Nude (location)	📷	📷					
Glamour	📷	📷					
Animals		📷					
On safari		📷					
Architecture	📷	📷		📷			
Travel	📷	📷	📷	📷	📷	📷	🔵
Travel (hot & humid)	📷	📷	📷	📷	📷		
Travel (cold)	📷	📷	📷	📷	📷		

84

LENSES						FILM							
Normal 50mm	Macro 55, 105, 200mm	35–70mm, Zooms 80–200mm	Telelenses 135–180, 200mm	Long lenses 300, 400, 500–1200mm	Special purpose	Kodachrome	50–100 ISO E6	200–400 ISO E6	Type B	Colour negative	Black and white 25–100 ISO	Black and white 125–1600 ISO	Special film
●	●	●	●			●	●		●	●	●	●	
		●	●	●		●			●			●	
●	●	●	●			●	●	●	●	●		●	
●		●	●			●	●	●	●	●		●	
●		●	●	●					●	●			
	●	●				●	●	●				●	
	●					●			●		●		
●	●					●		●	●	●		●	●
●	●					●					●	●	
	●		●						●			●	
		●	●	●					●			●	
			●	●	●	●	●			●	●	●	●
		●	●						●	●		●	
	●								●	●		●	
	●		●			●	●			●		●	
	●	●	●			●			●	●	●		
●		●	●			●	●	●				●	●
●		●	●	●		●	●			●		●	
	●	●		●	●	●	●			●		●	
		●	●	●	●				●	●		●	
●			●		●	●		●			●		●
●	●	●	●	●	●	●	●	●	●	●	●	●	●
●	●	●	●	●		●	●	●	●	●	●	●	
●	●	●	●	●		●	●	●	●	●	●	●	

Equipment chart □ 2

	TRIPODS					CASES		
	Normal	Heavy	Monopod	Tabletop unit	Clamps, beanbags	Aluminium case	Soft bag	Insulated film bag
Portraits (studio)	▲							
Portraits (location)	▲						▪	
Children							▪	
Weddings	▲		▲				▪	
Photojournalism	▲	▲	▲	▲	▲	▪	▪	▪
Out for the day			▲				▪	
Still life (studio)		▲						
Still life (location)	▲	▲				▪		
Close-up		▲						
Close-up wildlife							▪	
Sport	▲		▲				▪	
Landscape		▲				▪	▪	▪
Aerial							▪	
Marine								▪
Beauty	▲							
Nude (studio)	▲							
Nude (location)	▲					▪		
Glamour	▲					▪		
Animals		▲	▲		▲		▪	▪
On safari	▲	▲			▲	▪	▪	▪
Architecture	▲					▪		
Travel	▲		▲	▲	▲	▪	▪	▪
Travel (hot & humid)	▲							▪
Travel (cold)	▲		▲	▲				▪

| LIGHTS | | | METERS | | | | FILTERS | | | | | | ACCES-SORIES | |
Compact flash units	Strong bulbs	Reflectors	Spot/Gossen	Flash	Weston	Colour temperature	Polarizing	Warming	Graduated	Soft	Special effects	Correction filters	Cable release	Compass
●	●	●						●		●				
●		●					●	●	●	●	●			
●								●		●				
●			●				●			●				
●		●	●			●	●	●	●			●	A	A
●		●		●			●	●	●		●		A	A
		●	●	●									A	
●	●	●	●		●						●	●	A	
●		●	●	●							●		A	
●			●								●		A	
			●				●				●			
			●				●		●				A	A
			●				●							
●							●		●			●		
	●	●						●	●					
		●		●				●	●					
●		●				●	●	●		●		●		
		●				●	●		●			●		
●			●											
			●				●	●					A	A
	●			●			●		●	●			A	A
●		●			●	●	●	●	●	●	●	●	A	A
●		●			●		●	●	●			●		
●		●			●		●	●			●	●		

87

The system

Anyone just starting to take 35mm photography seriously needs to know how to build up a good camera system—a system which gives the maximum versatility.

So many manufacturers promote the technological or cosmetic aspects of their equipment that photography often seems to take second place and it is hard to sort out advice from advertising. The following suggestions for a system are based on picture-taking performance. Virtually all the pictures in the portfolio sections of this book can be taken with this set of equipment.

Many manufacturers offer a comprehensive range of equipment. A Nikon system is illustrated, but Canon, Leica, Olympus, Contax, Pentax, Rollei, Minolta and several others also supply complete 35mm camera systems with a similar range of lenses and other items.

Buy an automatic camera body with manual override. Check that the body is strongly built and ergonomically designed. The dealer may try and sell the body with a normal (50mm) lens, but the best buy for your first lens is a 35–70mm zoom with macro facility. This has the range to cope with most photographic needs; it is good for subjects from wide angle landscapes to portraits.

Modern quality lenses are sharp at any aperture, whether wide open or stopped down. It used to be thought that a lens would be sharper stopped down two stops from wide open, but this no longer applies.

Once you have your camera body and basic lens you can start to build a versatile system with a selection of lenses in different focal lengths.

Nikon F-801 (N8008)

24mm lens

1.4 teleconverter

35–70mm zoom lens

80–200mm zoom lens

300mm lens

The best second purchase is probably a 24mm lens. It has all the best wide angle qualities with little distortion and is an excellent lens for general photography.

Third should be an 80–200mm zoom lens. This is an ideal lens for carrying around on, say, a day out when the photographer does not want to be burdened with too much equipment. It is versatile and copes with a wide range of subjects from sweeping landscapes to intimate portraits.

A second camera body should be the fourth purchase in order to utilize the full complement of lenses, or when both colour and black and white films are being used. It can also be useful when speed is of the essence—it is quicker to change cameras than reload film.

The fifth item should be a 300mm lens, the first of the telelenses. It sees more than the naked eye and is good for photographing subjects such as sport and animals. It also foreshortens perspective, thus providing some interesting effects.

A sixth purchase to allow yet more adaptability should be a 1.4 teleconverter to turn the 300mm lens into a 450mm.

Of the other equipment necessary for the serious photographer the most important item is a good tripod. It allows pin-sharp pictures to be achieved when using slow shutter speeds and small apertures.

Putting such a system together is undoubtedly expensive and buying some items second hand can reduce costs. There are many reputable dealers and classified ads in the photographic press are a good source of equipment. Always test second-hand equipment thoroughly before buying.

In addition to the basic cameras and lenses the serious photographer should have a range of accessories, beginning with those illustrated below.

The following filters should be added to the beginner's system: 81A/B/C, 85A, 80B, polarizer, ND2, graduated, star and soft.

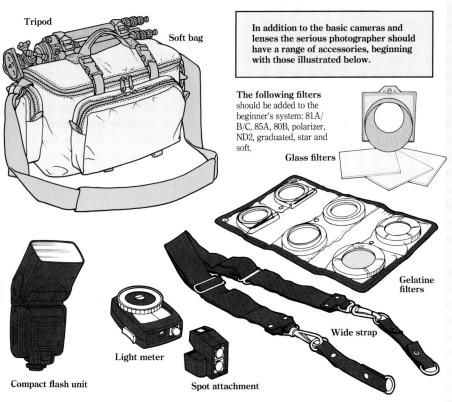

Tripod

Soft bag

Glass filters

Gelatine filters

Wide strap

Compact flash unit

Light meter

Spot attachment

Preparation

A systematic approach to photography depends as much on preparation and care of equipment as on the readiness and ability to take a picture. Everything from expensive cameras to the cheapest accessories must be kept in an orderly condition if good, clean, accurate pictures are to be made. Protect cameras and lenses from dust, moisture and extremes of temperature and keep them separate from darkroom equipment.

Cleaning equipment

Compressed cleaning air (1). Choose the ozone-friendly brands now available. When using, always hold the can upright or the air comes out as vapour, which smears the lens and takes time to clear. The small cans tend to vaporize even if held upright. Compressed air should be used sparingly on the lens elements and around the film path. Often a chip of film lodges behind the take-up spool. Remember that a camera is not a sealed unit and compressed air is as likely to blow dust in as blow it off.

WD40 (2). Use on tripods, camera case locks and hinges and on certain parts of

the camera to protect against damp and rust. Put a small amount on a piece of soft lens cloth and wipe the camera metalwork (never the inside or the glass). Use WD40 if taking the camera near the sea or out in the rain. It slows down the eroding effect of salt and water.

Aero-stat (3). An antistatic pistol used on the film and take-up spools and back pressure plate. It is important to use this with motor drives, which create static on fast rewind.

Lens tissue (4). Do not use the cleaning cloths recommended for spectacles; these are often impregnated with a greasy cleaning agent. If rubbed on the lens grease can give a star filter effect.

The best cleaner is a well-washed chamois leather (5). Use the cleaning liquid (6) on a cloth or tissue and wipe gently over the lens, but only if the compressed air has failed to remove the dust, or if there are oily smears on the lens. In some parts of the world, however, dust is so fine that only the fluid will remove it. Under these conditions fit a filter to the lens and keep it clean.

Never wash a filter. Most smears will

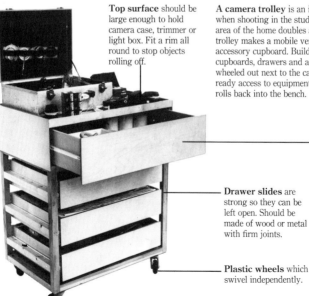

Top surface should be large enough to hold camera case, trimmer or light box. Fit a rim all round to stop objects rolling off.

A camera trolley is an invaluable piece of furniture when shooting in the studio or around the house. If an area of the home doubles as a make-shift studio, a trolley makes a mobile version of the camera and accessory cupboard. Build a workbench with cupboards, drawers and a fitted trolley, which can be wheeled out next to the camera set-up, providing ready access to equipment. After shooting the trolley rolls back into the bench.

Drawer slides are strong so they can be left open. Should be made of wood or metal with firm joints.

Plastic wheels which swivel independently.

Top drawer holds items such as household tools, staple gun, adhesive tape. Second drawer contains cameras and lens. Others hold film and miscellaneous equipment.

Trolley should be high enough to use surface without stooping and big enough to hold lots of equipment without getting in the way.

they are corroded, scrape with a knife or sandpaper. Never throw loose batteries into the camera bag; they can discharge on contact with any metal object, including other batteries. Buy batteries in plastic packs if possible and keep them wrapped until needed. If the only batteries available are not in sealed packs, ask the retailer to check the voltage.

When buying a camera check what batteries are required; some use lithium batteries made specially for that camera which can be difficult to find.

Maintenance
A leading camera service centre reports that more than 50 percent of camera malfunctions are due to worn-out batteries. Replace them regularly.

Other common camera faults are: plastic cogs wearing out quickly; compact camera mechanisms, such as shutter, wind-on, mirror lock, getting jammed by the smallest grain of sand; small screws falling out of complex cameras.

come off with a "huff" of breath. Always keep the back of the lens clean.

Brushes **(7)**. Blow brushes are manual versions of compressed air. They are good for general use and when travelling, but the bristles do get soiled easily. A sable paint brush **(8)** is useful for lenses and can be kept clean by simply washing gently in warm water. Use a stiffer brush **(9)** for camera body and metalwork, including the outside lens housing. Be sure to brush any grit away from the wind-on lever and small controls.

Cotton buds **(10)**. Use these to clean around the lens mount, controls and hinged back. Never touch the mirror with anything. Leave any cleaning to a specialist camera shop.

Batteries
In the new automatic cameras everything is battery powered. If the batteries fail, nothing happens. One of the first signs that batteries are running low is that the mirror fails to go back down properly after an exposure; this function takes more power than anything else.

Batteries have a built-in clock—they always fail when the stores are shut. Check batteries are working before going out with the camera and always carry spares. Keep batteries warm and clean. As a rule, do not touch terminals, but if

---

CHECKPOINTS
● Never oil the barrel of a lens. Oil seeps through and clogs the iris blades.
● If the camera is not used for long periods do not forget about it. Periodically run through a series of exposures—even without film.
● If the camera is in daily use have it checked over and serviced once a year. Most camera shops have electronic equipment to check the shutter speeds.
● If you have more than one camera and a selection of lenses in use, a camera mechanic can match the shutter speeds and aperture to within $\frac{1}{4}$ stop.
● Most faults with modern sophisticated cameras are operator malfunctions. PEOPLE DO NOT READ THEIR CAMERA MANUALS PROPERLY.

Checklist

Consistently good results depend largely on good habits. Most of the disappointments experienced when pictures come back from the laboratory can be avoided by making this checklist automatic.

If the film is changed in mid-roll, always make a note of the frame number when the film is unloaded and mark it on

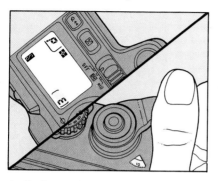

1. Check camera is not loaded, indicated by lack of tension on film advance lever on manuals. On automatics, E for empty appears on LED screen.

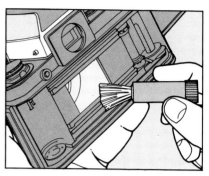

2. Check that the film path is free of dust, especially around the shutter. Check that there are no hairs caught in the shutter track.

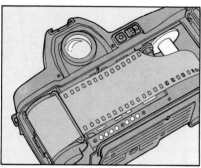

3. Check on automatics that film will automatically engage on take-up spool. On manuals check it is threaded into take-up spool.

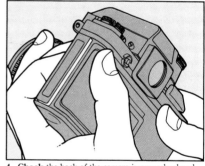

4. Check the back of the camera is properly closed. The slightest knock could open it and ruin the film.

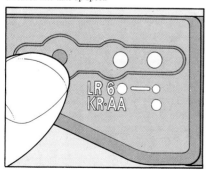

5. Check battery power. On many automatics there is a battery check button. If both LEDs light up when button is pushed, power is sufficient.

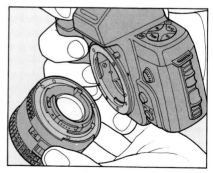

6. Check that the lens fitted to the camera is absolutely clean, particularly around the rear element.

the cassette or can. It is better to have a blank frame than a double exposure. Never *assume* that everything is alright. Check it, check it, CHECK IT with

the help of the following diagrams. Where there are two images in a square the top refers to automatic cameras, the bottom to manuals.

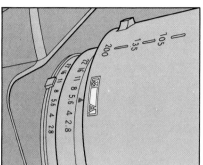

7. Check on automatics whether the lens is on manual, macro or autofocus. On both manual and automatics check lens is mounted properly.

8. Check that ISO (ASA) scale on the camera is set correctly for film in use and you know if it is over or under rated.

9. Check what film is in the camera, especially if it has not been used for a while.

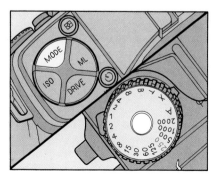

10. Check that there is no unwanted filter fitted to the front of the lens.

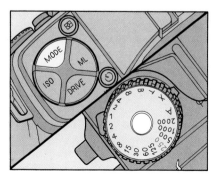

11. Check that an automatic camera is set on the right mode. Check that a manual is on the correct shutter speed.

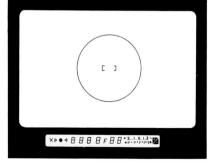

12. Check that the information in the screen of an automatic camera is realistic. Always be aware of the decisions the camera is making.

93

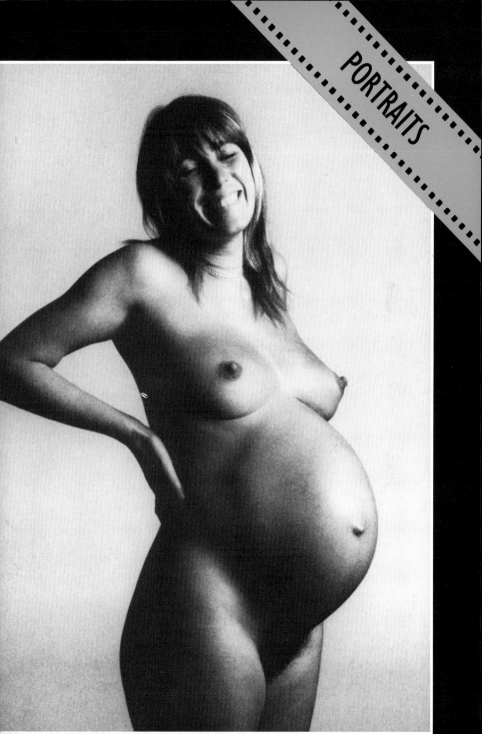

Portraits

The 35mm camera brings its own qualities to portrait photography—just as do the larger format cameras such as the Hasselblad and twin lens Rolleiflex.

Its speed of operation and small size make the 35mm the obvious choice for location portraits, or for spontaneous pictures when the photographer wants to be free of lots of cumbersome equipment. The high quality fast lenses do not need a lot of light to hold sharpness throughout a shot. All lenses have a creative potential for portraiture, but those most appropriate are the 90/105mm range, including the macro.

A 35mm camera is much less intimidating than larger format equipment. Most people, even models, are apprehensive when sitting for photographs and it is vital to help them feel relaxed before you start work.

Do not separate photography from the rest of your life. Most people have to relate to others in the course of their work, and have to make them feel at ease. Portraiture is little different except that over the duration of the sitting the photographer must produce a good picture.

Do not dither or flap around. You have to project an air of confidence and it helps if you know what you are doing.

The search for the true personality of the sitter makes portraiture one of the most fascinating aspects of photography. Have faith in first impressions but also be observant. Look at the face, hands, stature and carriage of the sitter—body language can reveal much about personality. Try and observe with discretion, especially if the subject is very nervous.

The facial lines of middle-aged and older people are not there by chance— they are the direct result of the lives they have lived. Do not try to change such characteristics but be kind when it matters.

Portrait photography takes several forms. In the studio, either a good likeness or a critical view can be achieved. When taking formal portraits, most photogra-

The simplicity of this daylight portrait allows the confident, self-assured personality of the model to shine through. A north-facing window provided a soft, even light; the model was leaning on a white surface against a white background.

The snapshot portrait, *right,* is the type of picture carried in millions of wallets to remind people of the ones they love. These pictures would never be considered art but bring more pleasure to more people than any other type of photograph. The snapshot portrait should never be dismissed as trivial.

phers attempt to make a sympathetic likeness of the subject. Use a tripod to give the sitter a constant point of reference. You can then move about and look at the sitter without inhibiting her.

Make sure the sitter knows there will be more than one exposure; several rolls might even be shot. If a subject feels particularly intimidated by the camera, shoot a roll or two in a throwaway manner but always have film in the camera. The best shot may come early on in the session, but if the camera is not loaded it will be lost.

Sculptor Andy Goldsworthy was photographed in his natural setting—outdoors with his work. The informal portrait shows not only the man but his relationship to what he has created.

We decided to take the photograph at midday when the circle on the side of the black slate sculpture appears white due to the angle of the sunlight—a feature of the work. This picture was a joint effort.

Keep talking to the sitter to establish eye contact. Always ensure the eyes are sharp even if other features are out of focus.

Environmental and reportage portraits out of the studio show people in less controlled situations and give an idea of their lives. Such pictures present the subjects in their world rather than just a facial likeness.

People do not always have to look at the camera. A successful portrait can be taken even if the subject is unaware of being photographed. Such shots are very difficult to take with anything other than a 35mm camera—the best camera for taking pictures of people going about their business, or unguarded moments.

The most universal type of photographic portrait is the snapshot. Snapshots are pictures of the ones we love. They are fond memories to be carried in the wallet and at their best represent a valid photographic form. Professional photographers generally find snapshots hard to take; they are too preoccupied with technique to be sufficiently involved with the situation.

Portraits

Knowing how to help subjects make the best of themselves is as important as understanding the lighting techniques and philosophy of portraiture.

When taking a portrait which is intended to flatter, start by putting the subject at ease. Often the act of giving subjects something to do toward the set-up has the effect of distracting them from their natural terror. If the subject is relaxed the portrait will be more successful.

To help subjects project the image they desire the photographer must have a sympathetic attitude toward people. With practice the eye will become more critical and speedily recognize faults that are better hidden or camouflaged.

Be aware of the graphic relationship between subject and surroundings. Patterned clothing and bold backgrounds can be used to good effect, but often they tend to detract from the point of interest—the subject.

Have plain black polo neck sweaters or T-shirts to hand. Most people look good in them and the face and hands stand out with no visual distractions. When shooting colour film choose clothing in plain colours that complement the subject's appearance and character.

Nervous tension is often revealed in the action of the subject's hands. Many people grip the chair or clench their fists. Try to get the subject to fold the arms, clasp the hands or put them flat on a table or their knees. If this does not work keep the hands out of the picture.

Candlelight is soft and warm in colour and is one of the most flattering and romantic of all portrait lights. The flickering, directionless light smooths out facial wrinkles. Take reflected readings off the face since the image flame will give an incorrect reading.

Watch out for neck wrinkles when shooting over the shoulder. If the head is tilted back and then turned to camera the neck will wrinkle. If the subject drops the head forward a little and then lifts it while turning to camera, wrinkles will be reduced.

Many subjects reveal their tension when being photographed by staring at the camera. Ask the subject to close his eyes, drop his chin onto the chest, then slowly lift the head and open the eyes. The stare will be gone.

To hide baldness, light the subject from the side and shoot from below the chin line. Lighting from above and shooting from forehead level gives unwanted prominence to the hair line.

To minimize a double chin, shoot from slightly above the head with the subject leaning forward, forcing him to stretch out the chin by looking up. Do not let him sit ramrod stiff with a forced smile and chin held in.

Tension around the mouth is a common sign of nervousness. Ask the subject to fill her cheeks with air and blow it out. This relaxes the mouth and the silliness of the act usually produces a genuine smile.

Encourage the subject to lean forward into the picture as a general rule. A positive attitude to the camera produces more dynamic portraits.

When photographing people with large noses use as long a focal length lens as possible. Long lenses compress perspective, wide angles exaggerate. Position the subject square to the camera and avoid throwing a shadow from the nose.

99

Portraits

While it is easy to record a likeness of a person it is much harder to make a visual statement of their personality. Photographers often need to think around their subject to make an interesting portrait. For instance, rather than just showing an architect in front of a building he has designed, try photographing him or her holding a model or drawings of the building.

One of the advantages of using a 35mm camera is that most people being photographed have no idea how much the lens sees of them. A wide angle lens can place people in among the symbols of their life and maintains a strong relationship between the camera and subject. A long lens can either isolate the subject from the background or bring the background up

behind them, establishing another relationship.

The many special effect techniques can add visual interest to a portrait, but should only be employed when relevant, not just as gimmicks. Study the lighting of great portrait paintings and learn from them. The best photographic portraits can make as important a visual statement as most paintings.

The shepherd belongs to the nomadic Guja tribe of northern India, descendants of the ancient biblical Syrians. The intention of the portrait was to show him looking like a biblical character. It is a set-up shot—although the tribe do carry lambs like this, it was placed there for the picture. A 300mm lens was used to keep a good distance from the shy subject.

Singer David Bowie was shot in action, using a 300mm lens, from the pit by the stage. Filled with guards and hysterical fans, the pit is a terrible place to work—a good picture was a just reward.

A group portrait normally requires careful composition and control. These men in Suffolk, England, however, were so perfectly grouped when spotted they were photographed just as they sat.

Children

Photographing children is a part of the overall enjoyment of family life. It should not be a special activity or made to seem over important, but just treated as great fun. Parents should be relaxed and confident with the camera, taking pictures of their children whenever the spirit moves them. If you fail today there is always tomorrow. Adopt this philosophy and many good shots will be made.

Photographing one's own child can be extremely rewarding and involves the parent in one of the great photographic themes. The great children pictures are those in which the photographer has recorded the world of the child, not just taken a likeness. Taking pictures of children can also be a most exasperating and frustrating experience. Looking back, the parent with a camera will remember as many near misses as a fisherman.

Children go through different stages, sometimes extrovert, sometimes shy. Never try to force children into being photographed when they are feeling shy. They resent it and may never feel comfortable in front of a camera again. Understanding and sympathy works much better than force.

In the real world children (especially babies and toddlers) have colds, rashes, spots and bad temper. Even under these conditions good pictures can be made which are interesting to look back on in later years.

There is no such thing as a special light for child photography, but many of the best pictures are shot in natural light. The absence of complicated lighting arrangements allows the photographer to concentrate on the actions and expressions of the child.

It is not just parents who like taking pictures of children. When travelling, for example, local children are often willing subjects and make memorable pictures.

In the studio
When taking pictures of other people's children find out the child's best time of

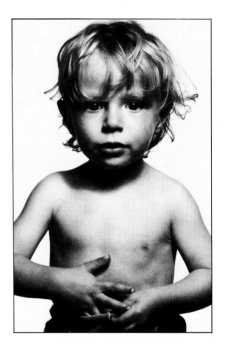

day and work round that. If a child always has a sleep after lunch it is no use trying to photograph her then. With very young children ask the mother or father to stand behind the camera with you so the child is looking at the parent.

Children are small people, not beings from outer space, so don't insult their intelligence. Be firm, polite and precise when giving directions. Children don't have to be handled with "kid gloves". It is often a good idea to let the child help with setting up a studio session. This helps them to feel relaxed and involved.

Never start the session until absolutely ready. When setting up the lights use an adult; a child's concentration does not last long. When the child is there do not waste time—especially if he or she is under six years of age. Have the camera ready and loaded, with the next roll out of the packet. Take meter readings in advance.

If the child is not interested, forget it. You will waste film and lose confidence. Don't ever panic—it is only a photographic session, not a summit meeting.

Children under the Christmas tree, *above*, with their favourite new toys make a perfect picture for the family album. This was shot on a 50mm autofocus lens and lit by flash bounced off the ceiling.

Three Kashmiri boys, *below*, display frank awe and curiosity when faced with camera equipment. In such situations let the children look at the camera, involve them and record their reactions.

Children

The biggest mistake people make when photographing children is to put the camera down too soon. Children have a talent for performing the moment the camera is put away. Be patient and stay around. If the camera is always there, the child will soon get used to it.

When photographing "world of the child" shots rather than simple portraits, set up a situation in which the child is sure to respond. Then back off. Allow them to become involved, then shoot.

The fact that the environment has been set up allows shots to be anticipated to some degree—easier than trying to follow totally spontaneous activity.

Try shooting from a kneeling position—the child's eye view. One

seldom sees pictures of children shot from their own level.

When shooting in the studio it can be a struggle to keep the child entertained. Try recording his own voice and playing it back; children are usually fascinated by the sound of their own voices.

Apart from all the basic techniques of portraiture, one of the most important factors in photographing children is the ability to follow focus. On all lenses bring the left hand down as the subject comes closer, and turn clockwise when the child moves away. Children move fast and follow focus is vital. An autofocus camera is ideal in this situation and will probably produce a better result than manual follow focus.

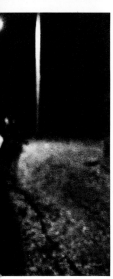

Photojournalism

The photojournalist remembers good pictures with pride but is inevitably haunted by the great ones missed.

The skill of photojournalism is to capture the essence of the human condition in pictures that will inform and clarify the minds of those who see them. The great news pictures and photo stories are a comment on the times in which they were taken and can have long lives.

The attitude of the photographer to his or her subject is of prime importance. Success may often depend on using common sense, but there are some basic techniques which the aspiring photojournalist might bear in mind.

1 Concentrate on the subject and always look for the poignant picture.

2 Be aware of what is going on around you and develop the knack of instinctively being where the picture will happen.

3 Have a personal response to the subject while maintaining sufficient detachment to spot the right picture.

4 Be ready to go to almost any lengths to get the picture.

5 Inspire faith in others so that they help you get what you want.

6 Keep pressure on oneself when the pictures are not happening. Often the best pictures happen just when you have thought of giving up.

7 Have a sound knowledge of photographic technique so that operating your camera becomes second nature.

8 Understand fully the properties of the film being used.

9 Never be put off by what may seem problems—mixed light sources, low light level, inaccessibility, for example. With patience and full command of techniques a problem can be turned into a creative advantage.

10 Remember that obtaining a picture is the objective. If you see the picture without the camera at your eye, you have probably missed it. The ability to anticipate action comes with experience.

Photojournalism can require a conscience as well as a camera. The shot of the boy being threatened, *above*, accompanied stories on children and violence. Bangladeshi "freedom fighters" taunt a prisoner, *left*, during the Indo-Pakistani war.

The intimate shot of the Queen in China, *preceding pages*, was obtained by using a 450mm lens.

"Some of the most compelling reportage pictures have been taken by photographers working with a journalist. A good journalist has a mind like a camera—that is, he thinks not only in abstract ideas and facts but also in images—and he can suggest situations to a photographer which he has "photographed" in his mind. A good photographer can see images through his lens which can best be described in words and these he passes to the journalist. Some of the finest reportage pictures and words stem from this rare overlapping of talents."
John Pilger
Foreign correspondent

"A photograph is as vital to a newspaper page as a news despatch. Like a written article, it should be informative and entertaining. It can grab a reader's attention faster than an article and almost as quickly as a headline. A good news photograph tells the news at a glance. It also can seduce the reader into examining the written word.

A reporter wants a photograph to report. A photograph should tell the reader of a place and of action and of people and their emotion. A photograph can set a scene and show the action of world events; tears, laughter, boredom, triumph and tragedy can be reported in words that take only minutes to read. A photograph can do the job in seconds— and make the impact last a lifetime. A good photograph is worth one word—impact."
Richard H. Growald
National Reporter, U.P.I.

Photojournalism

The crowd at an English race meeting, *above*, was shot on a 400mm lens, which foreshortens perspective and packs up the figures. The picture of the African woman is nothing until you notice the child's eyes. Look out for telling details.

CHECKPOINTS

- Ideally carry two automatic bodies, both with motor drive; 20mm, 28mm, 35mm and 300mm lenses and 80–200mm zoom; small flash, monopod and meter with spot attachment; a compact camera is also useful.
- In the camera bag carry fast black and white and colour film, rolls of type B colour and whatever else you feel happy using. Take what you are likely to need but don't try to carry more than you can run with.
- Wide angle lenses allow the photographer to come in close to the subject—reaction to a closely positioned camera can sometimes add a vital element to a shot. Autofocus can be invaluable when it is important to shoot quickly.

Photojournalism is about photographing people's lives, telling their stories. The Pope, *above*, is obviously an interesting subject, but the fact it is a special day for those people involved makes this a good reportage picture. A genial smile reveals something of the personality beneath the aggressive attire of the punk, *below left*. When taking a picture of the Seoul police, *below*, the photographer tried to see beyond their image as law enforcers and show them as fellow humans in uniform.

Photojournalism

The photo story is a stimulating and valid assignment for the photojournalist, allowing the opportunity for vivid insights into the human condition. The versatile 35mm camera is the most appropriate equipment for capturing the definitive moments of a story—these pictures illustrate a day in a teaching hospital.

The pictures in this photo story succeed because they are varied. They range from general shots to details, and include moments of drama and tension as well as joy and even humour.

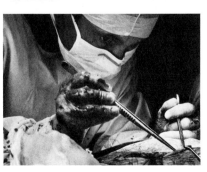

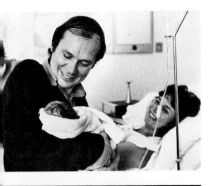
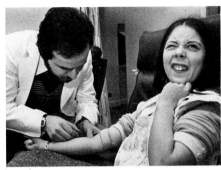

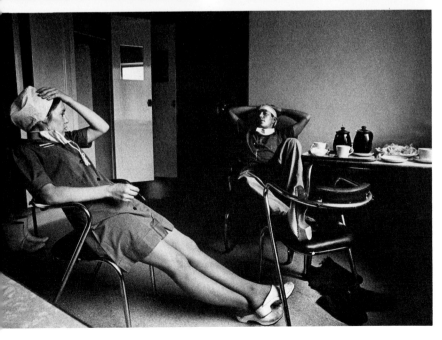

Photojournalism

The services of the photojournalist are often called upon by design groups to record a company's activities. The picture that successfully defines the relationship between worker and machine or conveys the atmosphere and activity in the workplace may take a day or more to stage manage; or may be taken quite spontaneously.

A good test of such a picture is to show it to the working people in the photograph. If they say, "yes, that's how it is", then the photographer has gone a long way to creating a convincing picture.

The barrel testing routine in a Californian winery, *right*, was shot for a corporate brochure. As well as recording the daily activity it was important to convey the brand identity in a natural way.

The scene in a Hong Kong tailor's shop, *below,* shows people engrossed in their work—no glamour, no fuss but a picture that takes you right into the midst of those workers' lives.

A welder in action, *above*, was shot on a 300mm lens with an exposure of 1/15 second to record the sparks and smoke. The camera was mounted on a tripod. The result is a dramatic picture that conveys the intensity and precision of such work.

The Yorkshire blacksmith's shop, *right*, was photographed in daylight on fast (800 ISO) film; lighting the scene would have destroyed the atmosphere of the interior. A number of shots were taken in order to catch the exact moment of a blow to the horseshoe.

Weddings

For many couples their wedding day is one of the most important of their lives. Don't offer to take the official photographs of such a momentous occasion unless you are completely confident of what you are doing—confident of your equipment, the light conditions and of your ability to handle people and work fast.

If the formal wedding pictures are left to the local specialist who uses a larger format camera, the 35mm photographer is free to record all the unguarded, informal moments of the day. The best pictures may well be taken long after the official photographer has gone home. It is a friendly family time, when everybody is excited and far more interested in talking to long-lost relatives than paying any attention to a photographer.

Be firm and pleasantly dictatorial if necessary to get the pictures you want; in years to come people will thank you for your persistence.

The bride's mother, *preceding pages*, adjusting the veil that she wore on her own wedding day. Photographed just before leaving the bride's home with a 35mm lens and fast film.

The couple emerging from the church, *top left*, is a must to photograph, but watch for problems caused by the contrast between the groom's dark suit and bride's white dress and expose for the faces. Take an incident light reading in front of the doorway before the couple come out and work to that. An automatic camera would expose for the white dress and faces would be too dark.

This lively informal portrait, *left*, was taken with an 80–200mm zoom lens. After the ceremony when everyone is crowded outside the church and movement is difficult a zoom lens helps the photographer get varied shots without too much running around.

Signing the register, *above*. Hand flash was bounced off the ceiling but on a slow shutter speed to kill the hard flash shadows.

Choose your position then instruct guests to throw confetti when you give the word. Use a slowish shutter speed so the confetti is slightly blurred.

Weddings

When photographing a wedding, plan a shooting schedule in advance. List the aspects of the event you need to cover and try to photograph them all. Some obvious shots are of the bride dressing, her arrival at the church, the ceremony, signing the register, family groups, cutting the cake, and leaving for the honeymoon. Other shots might include the presents, a posed portrait of the bride, the guests arriving.

At the reception a range of different—often humorous—subjects present themselves. Photograph the funniest telegram, the oldest relative or father dancing. Receptions are usually indoors and modern automatic cameras work well in these situations. With the camera on automatic and the latest flash-on-camera technology, satisfactory results are achieved effortlessly and you can concentrate on spotting interesting pictures.

Instead of using transparency film, shoot colour negative film and have a quick set of machine prints done at a one-hour processing booth. This is fast and simple and, since people will want prints anyway, it makes it easier for them to make their selection. Any enlargements or special prints can be done later.

Still life

Form, texture and the relationship of one object to another are prime concerns in still-life photography. Equally important considerations are the lighting of those objects and the overall composition of the picture. Still-life photographers have been known to take days arranging items, striving for the simplicity of a composed, harmonious picture.

Professional photographers often use large format cameras for still life, but amateurs can achieve good results on 35mm with much less effort. Mount the camera on a tripod, so you are free to compose your picture and rearrange the objects until you have the desired effect. Use slow film and bracket exposures— you might get some unexpected and perhaps pleasing results.

The objects in a still life, although appearing in one dimension, must have body and substance and this impression can be created by lighting. Although the lighting is under the total control of the photographer, nothing is original. All artificial lighting effects are imitations of natural light, so study the effects of daylight on various surfaces. When re-creating an effect with studio flash, use the modelling lights to see what the flash is going to do.

Top backlighting makes objects stand out from the background, separating one from the other and giving good 3D light around the edges.

Diffused light is better than hard, raw light for most subjects so use a diffuser.

The larger the light source the better the light. One light source with several reflectors to put the light back into the set can be used to hold natural detail in the shadows. This is generally better than lighting the dark areas of the picture with separate lights.

The collection of glasses, *preceding pages*, was shot on a 105mm macro lens. They were placed on a sheet of glass against a white infinity background running from the edge of the set, under the glass, down to the ground and back up in a loop. The loop area was lit by (1), set at two stops over the general reading. Extra power was needed to "light out" the back edge of the sheet of glass. (2) lit the liquid.

A glass full of liquid picks up reflections, so keep the area behind the camera dark and free from reflective objects.

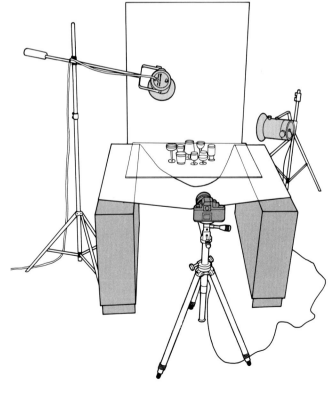

The Cartier objects
were placed on a piece of
black slate which had
been rubbed down with
oil to create some
reflections. The light
was pushed through a
double layer of white
Rosco tissue paper. Not
only did the light
illuminate the objects,
but the reflecting
surfaces of the objects
are picked out by the
large area of white
paper.

The black velvet
absorbed all unwanted
light on the left side of
the set. A piece of white
polystyrene was used as
a general background.

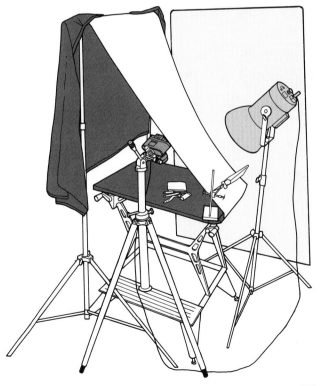

Still life

Great still-life shots were being taken long before the invention of electronic flash with the best of all lights—daylight. The mobility of the 35mm camera enables the photographer to take still lifes anywhere.

Pictures may come from arrangements of favourite objects or may be pure chance. Take these pictures quickly and simply, or if there is time use a tripod, which allows more opportunity for deliberation and minor adjustments in the relationship between objects.

Still lifes can be used to add detail to any series of pictures, and can sometimes say more about a subject than conventional shots. They need not always be arrangements—a close-up of a tiny detail can make an attractive picture and gives that detail its own importance.

A detail, such as this car mascot, can make an interesting still life. Even though such a shot does not have to be arranged it requires just as much care. Make sure the subject is sharp and peripheral items are out of focus or eliminated.

CHECKPOINTS
● Use retort stands to hold mirrors for reflecting light into dark areas.
● Black velvet and sheets of white opaque plastic make useful backgrounds.
● Have sheets of coloured card, especially black, white, silver and gold, available for use as reflectors. Sheet glass on top of black velvet creates one very good reflected image.
● When photographing a bottle of red wine or port, dilute the liquid or light will not penetrate. If ice cubes are required in a shot use plastic ones—real ice melts too quickly.
● Take extra care with lighting and make-up if a model's hands are to be included in a picture; they can easily look like claws or chicken legs.

Black and white still life photography deals with texture, shape and the relationship of objects to each other and to their background. Colour tends to distract from these elements.

Before taking a still life consider every part of the picture in the viewfinder and create a balanced, pleasing composition.

The simplicity of the apples on a pewter plate, *right*, is deceptive; the composition took some time to perfect and each apple was positioned with care. The shot was lit by simulated daylight, created by a grilled box light softened by several sheets of tracing paper. This lighting gave the apples roundness and volume.

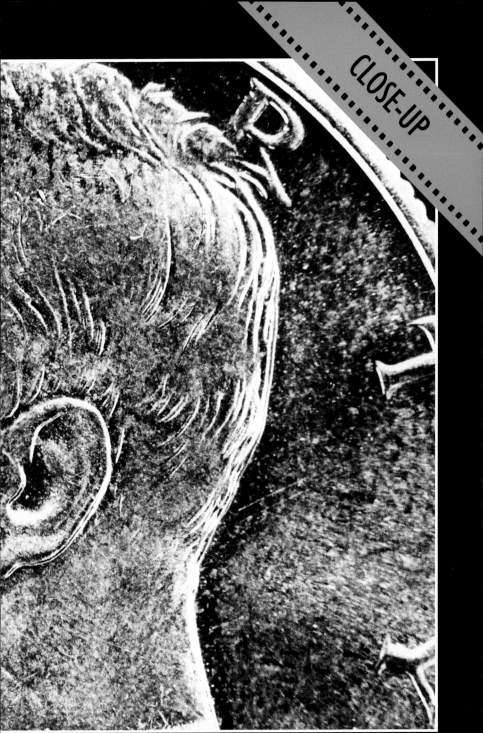

Close-up

Coming in close on small objects or details can produce interesting and revealing pictures. To shoot moderate close-ups, use a macro lens or close-up supplementary lenses. For greater magnification, use extension rings or a bellows attachment, both of which mount between camera and lens.

Since bellows and extension rings take the lens farther from the film plane, there is some loss of light, which can cause exposure problems. Extension rings have exposure factors engraved on them; bellows exposure is calculated by the length of extension. Electronic cameras, however, will gauge the exposure for you if set on aperture priority.

Providing sufficient light is a problem in close-up work; the closer the lens comes to the subject, the narrower the depth of field. There are two alternatives—long exposures or flash.

When shooting close-ups with a long exposure, make sure that the subject is completely stationary and that the camera is securely mounted and will keep steady. Tungsten light provides good constant illumination for studio work. Use mirrors, foil or white card to bounce light in between subject and lens at an oblique angle.

Outside, when shooting something such as a flower, use a ring flash or a small compact flash. These will freeze the movement from the wind and allow the lens to be stopped right down for maximum depth of field. Take a silver reflector and a piece of white paper to use in combination with the flash; it will throw a shadow, which may need to be softened. The ring flash provides a shadowless light so no reflector is necessary.

Electronic cameras have made flash-lit close-ups much easier—the amount of flash necessary when using an autofocus macro lens is automatically calculated.

The camera was mounted on an inverted tripod in the set-up for the coin picture. Tungsten lights were used with diffusers and barn doors. A reflector on one side of the coin and black card on the other side gave modelling.

When shooting a close-up of a flat object, such as the coin, make sure that both camera and subject are squared up. Use a spirit level.

The shot of a JFK coin was taken on a 55mm macro lens after experimenting with reflectors to pick up a glint in the eye.

The same lens was used with an M extension ring. Numbers on rings are exposure factors—2 requires one stop increase.

The M ring was replaced with K rings for this shot. The factor was 4, demanding an increase of two stops exposure.

Greatest magnification was achieved with a bellows fitted to the same lens. Exposure factors still apply but bracket shots.

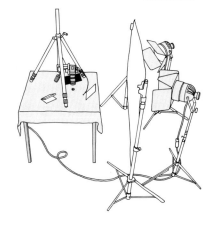

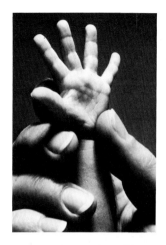

The baby's hand was photographed on an 80–200mm zoom fitted with a 0.5 supplementary lens—a useful combination for tight cropping on moving subjects. Flash was reflected from above by an umbrella.

The hyacinth was shot on a 55mm macro lens at f16, with a backlight from each side and fill-in light from front.

The eye was shot with a 105mm macro and lit by ring flash mounted onto the front of the lens, *below right.*

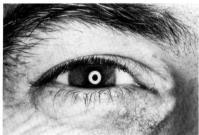

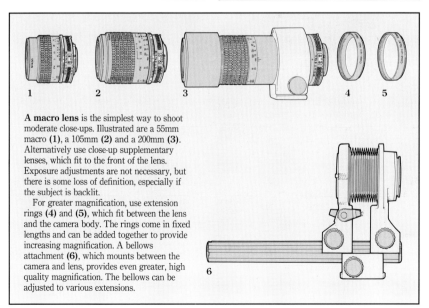

A macro lens is the simplest way to shoot moderate close-ups. Illustrated are a 55mm macro **(1)**, a 105mm **(2)** and a 200mm **(3)**. Alternatively use close-up supplementary lenses, which fit to the front of the lens. Exposure adjustments are not necessary, but there is some loss of definition, especially if the subject is backlit.

For greater magnification, use extension rings **(4)** and **(5)**, which fit between the lens and the camera body. The rings come in fixed lengths and can be added together to provide increasing magnification. A bellows attachment **(6)**, which mounts between the camera and lens, provides even greater, high quality magnification. The bellows can be adjusted to various extensions.

Landscape

Taking a successful photograph of a dramatic and beautiful landscape is one of the most challenging experiences for the 35mm photographer.

The major difficulty when using a 35mm camera to photograph a landscape is how to do justice to a huge vista on a small piece of film. There is a big difference between looking at a small picture on a viewer and projected on a big screen.

Scale is important in landscapes. Vistas look most impressive if there is something to relate to, such as a person, a house or a car. Panoramic shots should include foreground detail to catch the attention and then sweep the eye into the background of the picture.

A fishing village in southern Turkey, *left*, was photographed on a 35mm wide angle lens. This copes well with the rounded shapes of the boats in the foreground while keeping plenty of detail in the village in the background.

This impressive landscape in the Himalayan foothills, *right*, was also taken on a 35mm lens. The figure and campsite in the foreground underline the immense scale and grandeur of the scene.

The Tuareg, leading his three camels, makes this picture of a flat, stony area at the heart of the Sahara Desert.

Northern Portugal photographed during a lull in a thunderstorm, *preceding pages*. A 35mm lens was used with a graduated filter to accentuate the sky. The camera position had been selected in advance, but a heavy, dramatic sky was wanted to emphasize the mood of the location—site of a decisive battle during the 18th-century Peninsular Wars.

Landscape

Many beginners think that the wide angle is *the* landscape lens, but telephoto lenses, especially the 300mm, are also effective. When this lens is focused on infinity, the landscape is compacted into the picture and is rich in shapes. From a high vantage point on a clear morning a view of more than 150km (90mi) can easily be seen. To get such a scene into a picture to take home with you is worth all the effort.

Choose your position and lens with care. Many of the great landscape painters cheated. They moved rock outcrops, even mountains, a few inches on the canvas to make the composition work. Photography may lie a little but it doesn't cheat.

Graduated filters are useful to hold detail in the sky while retaining foreground interest. Polarizing or red filters on extreme wide angle lenses also add drama to the sky.

It is frustrating to be driving along in fantastic photographic weather, such as pre- or post-thunderstorm light, and not

Tanzania. Shot at midday with a 20mm lens and a red filter fitted to emphasize clouds. The truck arriving at the point of converging perspective becomes the focal point of the picture. Expansive landscapes such as this need something in the picture to catch the eye.

have a subject to photograph. Keep a good contour map in the car so you have some idea of the lie of the land and interesting features that might be worth investigating. Sunsets always help a landscape picture, but they disappear fast. Use a compass so you can work out where the ball of the setting sun is going to drop that evening.

A keen landscape photographer will learn to interpret weather patterns. In some parts of the world the weather is very predictable and not a problem, but, if it is changeable, use it. For an interesting series of pictures, try photographing a favourite landscape at intervals throughout the day from dawn to dusk. Choose a time of year that usually has a varied weather pattern.

An aerial shot of a château surrounded by vineyards in the Cognac area of France makes a graphic landscape with plenty of central interest. Being airborne gives the photographer a privileged view of the subject but little time to compose the picture.

The standing stones at Callanish on the Isle of Lewis, Outer Hebrides, *below*, were shot on a Widelux camera.

CHECKPOINTS

● Many photographers prefer to use black and white film for landscapes because the print is tangible. The grain and tones in a black and white print are also in harmony with the natural textures of rock, grass, lakes, mountains, sky and clouds.

● Colour landscapes in *National Geographic* magazines often include a back view of the photographer in his "special issue" red jacket. The eye goes straight for the red then wanders around the picture, taking it all in.

● Take a selection of lenses and filters when photographing landscapes and a steady tripod. A spirit level helps make compositions with level horizons.

● A Widelux camera or panoramic tripod head enables the largest vistas to be photographed.

● Carry a compass and binoculars. Do not be lazy and just shoot out of the car window—you are unlikely to get interesting shots. Leave the vehicle and walk around, looking for the best possible camera angles.

Aerial

From the air the world becomes one huge and incredible graphic design. Familiar cities and landscapes become a series of shapes made of light and shade.

If flying in a light aircraft or helicopter, brief the pilot on your needs before take-off. Explain what you want to photograph and the angles from which to approach the subjects. Ask the pilot to let you know where the aircraft's shadow will be. Ask him, too, to make rudder turns rather than flap turns, which cause the plane to bank steeply. Rudder turns keep the aircraft on a more even keel.

The best time to shoot pictures from an aircraft is early morning (up to two hours after sunrise), when the light is fresh and clean, and late afternoon (two hours before sunset), when the shadows are once again getting longer and the light is full of colour.

Unless the sun is catching a bright, reflective surface, such as water or glass, and throwing a strong highlight, exposures should be easy. Take an incident light reading of the light falling on the ground and expose accordingly. If it is a hazy day, underexpose slightly. On clear days the atmosphere tends to make colours appear cold; use an 2A or an 81 series filter. Orange filters are effective with black and white film. Use polarizers to cut reflected light, especially in the heat of the day.

Bracket exposures to cover all possible effects of design. Since the subject is a long way from the camera use the sharpest possible film. Kodachrome is good although it may be too slow for some occasions. Remember that aircraft vibrate considerably so use the fastest shutter speeds. Ideally, shoot at 1/500 second, never slower than 1/250 second.

Aerial photography from light aircraft is a pursuit limited to specialists and those lucky enough to know pilots, but there is also potential for picture taking from scheduled aircraft.

The most common problem when shooting through the window of an airliner is the intrusion of reflections on the inside window. These can usually be eliminated by cupping the hand around the front of the lens and pressing that against the window. A rubber lens hood can also cut out the light effectively. If you can do so without disturbing other passengers, throw an airline blanket over head and shoulders to cut out all chance of reflections.

The bold pattern made by the combine harvester working a field, *left*, was shot on a zoom lens with fast shutter speed. The zoom allows some "fine tuning" of the picture.

Manhattan, New York, *right*, shot from a helicopter during a sightseeing trip. A wide angle lens was used. Its slight distortion makes the buildings appear to surge upward, adding dynamism to the picture.

The oil rig, *preceding pages*, was shot with a 2A filter to accentuate the colour of the sunset.

MARINE

Marine

Photographing underwater is completely different from working on dry land. Unless you know exactly what you are doing, underwater is a dangerous place to be.

The Nikonos underwater camera, or the special housings which are available to take any type of 35mm camera, can be used without having to dive deep. Exciting pictures are to be had from shooting on the surface, half in and half out of the water (as in the picture on the preceding pages), or even from the shore or in a swimming pool.

Conditions in water are never consistent. Whether in ocean, lake, stream or swimming pool, the biggest photographic problems are those of exposure and colour rendition. Colour negative film can be useful for underwater work since some colour problems can be corrected at printing stage.

Much light is reflected off the surface and even with specialist underwater exposure meters, accurate readings are hard to achieve. Light is filtered through the water, often causing readings to be

about $\frac{1}{3}$ stop underexposed. Open up between $\frac{1}{4}$ and $\frac{1}{2}$ stop over the meter reading.

Electronic flash is essential in murky conditions, but much of the light bounces off minute particles suspended in the water. The key to good pictures is to keep the distance between camera and subject to a minimum and bracket exposures.

Use colour correction filters to help capture the great range of underwater colours. Clean sea water gives a bluish-green to greenish-blue cast, depending on the clarity and depth of the water, the type of sea bed and colour of the sky. Hot and cold currents also create differences in colour. Swimming pool water usually gives a blue cast.

Recording the warm colours in the red-orange range is the greatest difficulty. The use of filters is often purely experimental. Begin with a 10 Red working up to a 40 Red for the greenish-blue and try yellow filters from 10 upward for the bluish casts. Near the surface the 30 Red is most useful. Seacors Sea Filter I is also a good general purpose colour correction

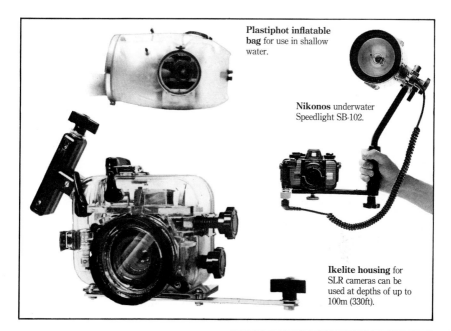

Plastiphot inflatable bag for use in shallow water.

Nikonos underwater Speedlight SB-102.

Ikelite housing for SLR cameras can be used at depths of up to 100m (330ft).

filter for underwater photography.

Filters that screw directly onto the lens must be fitted underwater to allow a liquid surface to meet both elements. An air pocket will cause distortion, and the difference in pressure may also crack the filter. Lens hood filter holders are not attached directly to the lens element so this does not apply.

The lenses available for the Nikonos camera are all comparatively wide angle since refraction underwater makes images appear bigger. They also necessitate working closer than normal to the subject to reduce diffusion of the image caused by light scatter. The extra depth of field is useful when shooting under low light levels.

Interesting underwater photographs can be obtained without using scuba equipment. Use a snorkel in shallow water. A wet suit can be vital in some locations—lakes and mountain streams can be extremely cold, and even in tropical waters a wet suit offers protection from sharp rocks, coral reefs and jellyfish stings.

CHECKPOINTS

● Mistakes underwater can be fatal. Before diving, learn about the physical and psychological hazards. Never dive alone. Once engrossed in photography, it is all too easy to drift away and into danger.

● Protect cameras from direct sun. Apart from adversely affecting the film and shutter mechanism, heat will dry out the grease on the waterproofing seal. After shooting wash the camera out thoroughly and re-grease the seals.

● Rough water reflects light off the surface, and ripples cause readings to fluctuate. Work out an average.

● Light reflected off a sandy bottom gives about one extra stop as a general rule.

● Shoot close to the subject. The ideal distance is one-fifth of total visibility—in 15m (50ft) visibility, shoot at 3m (10ft).

Beauty

Beauty photography differs from other types of portraiture in that the photographer wishes to depict women at their most glamorous and romantic. This image of womanhood is specifically aimed at women, rather than men, and has to appeal to female fantasies. The photography, which must be tasteful, requires the painstakingly clinical attitude of the still-life photographer. The top beauty photographers are highly skilled technicians, able to bring the right look and pose from the model at the decisive moment.

To achieve the shot on the preceding pages, an 80–200mm zoom lens was used, fitted with a Hasselblad Softar No. 1 filter, exposed at f11. A gold umbrella was covered with tissue paper and placed right over the lens. The background was pale green Colorama paper, lit from each side to make it smooth and even.

The model was sitting at a card table, on which she could lean her elbows and take up different poses in comfort. A white card was used on the table to bounce the light back into the shadows on the face.

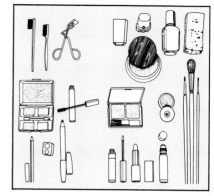

Some knowledge of the application of make-up is essential to the beauty photographer who must represent subtle cosmetic hues. Professionals use make-up artists, but amateurs should learn as much as possible themselves.

The basic equipment illustrated above includes:

Eyebrow brush	Sponge for base
Eyelash comb	Translucent powder
Eyelash curlers	Dip stick lipstick
Eye shadow	Tube lipstick
Mascara	Lip gloss
Kohl pencil	Lip brush
Pencil sharpener	Powder blusher
Eye shadow pencil	Cream blusher
Concealer	Blusher mop
Fluid base	Eye shadow brush

CHECKPOINTS

● Foundations are not masks. They make a good skin look better, a poor skin healthier. Dry skin needs thicker foundations; greasy skin needs fluid.

● Concealers are invaluable for covering dark shadows and blemishes. Anything made lighter stands out—anything made darker will recede.

● Blend all make-up well. For the best effects use professional make-up brushes. These are usually larger and fluffier than the brushes that come with most make-up products and much more efficient. Eye make-up brushes are tapered or chiseled depending on their purpose.

● Cover the skin with talc before applying quick-tanning cream so that the uncovered areas are visible.

● For eyes, apply basic cover first. If using pencils, apply on top of the base. If using powder, lighten the eyelid with translucent powder first so the shadow will set better. Emphasis can be applied with eyeliner; use only a thin line and blend it into the lash roots.

● Use bounced light off reflectors or umbrellas to make the face shadowless.

● A soft focus filter with the lens stopped down smoothes the skin.

● Experiment with other filters. A 2A or 81A, B or C plus a 5 Red will give a warm glow to skin tones.

● Cut out pictures of beautiful girls from magazines and keep them. Try to copy or adapt the ideas you like.

1   2   3

1 Base make-up. Use concealer to cover dark shadows under the eyes and blemishes. Apply fluid make-up with a damp sponge and concealer with a brush. Always use a base as close to natural skin tone as possible. Using a sponge gives smoothest texture. Blend away down neck and under chin to avoid a hard line.

2 Define the eye with a pencil and blend up into the brow bone with a brush to complement the shape of the eye. Choose a colour that suits the model's hair and eyes. Natural colours such as browns and pinks

are best. Stay clear of bright blues and greens, which can appear as bright blobs. The eyes are usually the focal point, and effective beauty pictures depend on eye contact between photographer and model.

3 Put translucent powder over the eyelids, then apply more colour with powder shadow. This defines the shape of the eye and deepens the colour. Apply mascara—water soluble is best—and use an eyelash comb to separate the lashes. Mascara helps open up the eyes. Make sure there are no blobs clinging to the lashes.

4   5   6

4 Apply translucent powder all over the face to remove shine. Then apply blusher on the cheekbones to define them and shape the face. Darken under cheekbones and lighten the top. Blend the blusher away to eliminate hard edges.

5 Outline lips with a red pencil first to define the shape. Fill this in with a slightly lighter lipstick; use a small, flat brush for best results. Use a touch of lip gloss on the bottom lip only to add highlight. Extend the line of a small mouth slightly. With a wide mouth, keep inside the line and use lighter colours. Finally,

hold a clean tissue against the lips and press lightly to remove any excess lipstick; peel away carefully.

6 Uncurl or dress the hair. Use a hair drier, blow heater or just flap a piece of card to give the hair life, then arrange to flatter the model's face. Electric rollers give the hair body and sleekness if that is the desired effect. Unless it has to be cut, do hair after make-up so it is not disturbed. Hair which is slightly greasy shows highlights better than dry hair. Freshly washed hair photographs badly—wisps stand out and look strawlike and untidy.

Nudes

A difficult subject to photograph well, nudes are all too easy to shoot badly.

The popular image of an extraordinarily beautiful Venus or Adonis waiting in front of the camera, of whom a failed picture would be impossible, is just a fantasy. The plain truth is that there are few perfect bodies—most have blotchy skin and lumps in the wrong places. Once this has been accepted nude photography becomes an exercise in creative lighting technique.

Always bear in mind that a human body is a collection of round shapes. Never light the body front-on since this will flatten those round shapes. Instead, light from above or on one side and use reflectors where necessary. The body must be lit to throw the imperfections into shadow or away from the camera. Arrange the pose carefully so that the model's best features are toward the camera.

When photographing a nude subject (even if the model is a friend), keep the atmosphere casual and relaxed. It is most important to keep the room or studio warm. Cold skin does not photograph well and blue blotches and goose bumps are not considered attractive. Assuming that the photographer has clothes on, the temperature should be slightly too warm for him or her. To make nipples stand erect apply an ice pack.

Models should not wear underclothes or other tight clothing for several hours before a session as elastic on socks, panties and bras leaves unpleasant marks. These take a long time to fade away so insist, tactfully, that models wear loose clothing only.

Never bother to attend group photo sessions with a shared model. These vulgarize the true spirit of nude photography and are hopeless for getting a beautiful picture.

The two shots on the preceding pages were taken against Colorama continuous background paper which had been sprayed with paint. The nude was lit with two front/side lights bounced off umbrellas covered with tissue. The face was backlit by another lamp with snoot.

The model stood in a plastic paddling pool, while an assistant on a stepladder poured warm water over her from a watering can fitted with a shower nozzle. The spotlight at the back was used to highlight the water and steam.

The female nude reclining on a mattress, *above,* was lit by a single light source bounced off a gold-coloured umbrella covered with tissue. By using an 80–200mm zoom lens, fitted with Softar and 81B filters, an almost abstract effect was achieved.

The male nude, *below,* was photographed to create a strong sculptural impression. His body was rubbed with baby oil to make the skin glow and accentuate the muscular form. A 300mm lens was used to isolate him from the background.

Pin-ups

The glamour photographer must first of all make the model feel fantastic.

The fact that a pretty girl agrees to pose for pin-up pictures usually indicates that she wants to be extrovert and look sexy and glamorous. It is up to the photographer to release her inhibitions and draw that look out of her. A good picture will not be achieved by being boorish and tasteless or trying to exploit the model.

Try and capture on film the image which a girl would present to the mirror in her room. Encourage her to pose so that she feels good, then adjust the pose to fit the shot.

Lighting should suit the model. Use strong midday sun or flash for an overtly sexy woman; a softer light for a quieter, more restrained girl.

Choose clothes carefully to suit the model. If she has great legs, show them; if beautiful breasts, show them. If she's got it, help her flaunt it!

A stretched-out pose
flatters the body of the
model, *left*. A 180mm
lens was used with a
polarizing filter to hold
the intensity of the gold
swimsuit and the suntan.
Such shots are best kept
simple for maximum
impact.

**A 35mm lens was
used to elongate** the
girl's figure, *right*. The
background is a lace net
curtain and a sheet of
Rosco paper was used as
a reflector to fill in the
shadows. The
backlighting is
sympathetic to the
rounded shapes. 81A
and 5R filters were used
to flatter and warm skin
tones.

Pictures of couples,
left, can also make
glamour shots and can
be fun to do. The shot
did not appear like this
to the eye—there was
plenty of detail in the
people and the water.
The gold shaft of light
from the sunset attracted
the photographer. By
exposing for this light
the couple were
underexposed by three
stops and reduced to
silhouettes. After
reducing the shot to
basic shapes the models
were carefully positioned
until seen in profile. If
using an automatic
camera override the
controls and expose for
the highlights to achieve
a silhouette effect.

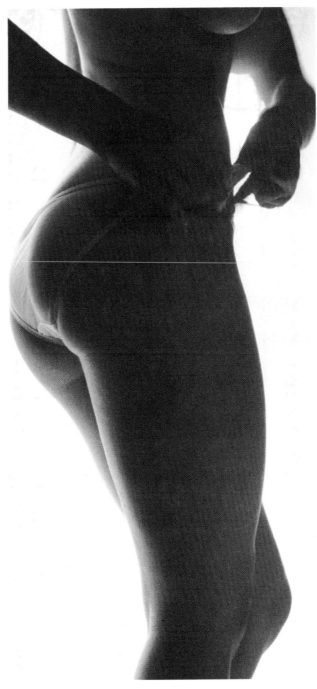

157

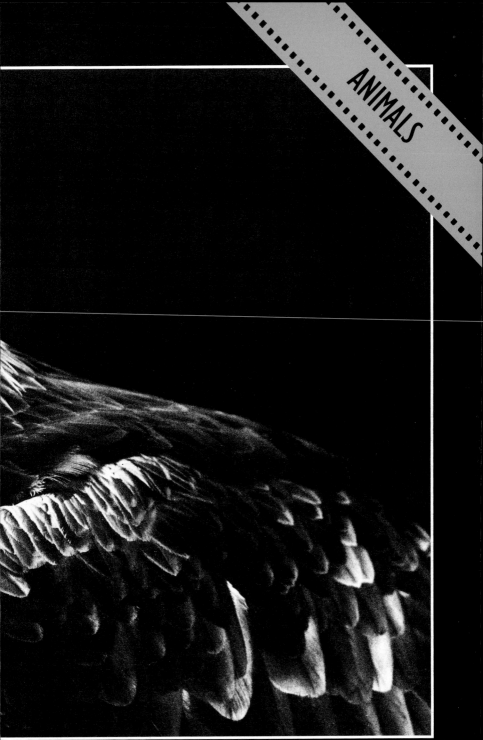

Animals

Great wild animal shots require patience and dedication as well as some knowledge of wildlife. The best shots are seldom the result of luck but are mostly taken by specialists who spend their lives photographing animals. Each photograph may take days of waiting for just the right moment.

The amateur should not be put off, however. Wonderful pictures can be had with a combination of patience, concentration, luck and the right equipment.

A 200mm lens is used like a normal lens in wide open spaces. A 300mm is the minimum length telelens. A 400mm or 1000mm is the most useful.

To take really good pictures of wildlife

a photographer needs to know a certain amount about animal behaviour to help him or her anticipate action. A naturalist's sensitivity can be as important as photographic technique.

On safari the best pictures are usually shot early in the morning or late in the evening: that is when the animals tend to be most active.

Once an animal has been located (with the help of a good guide), total concentration is the vital factor. Keep the eye to the camera and constantly check focus until the animal moves into the right position. Autofocus is invaluable for animal photography, leaving the photographer free to concentrate on the picture.

The golden eagle, *preceding pages,* was photographed in a bird sanctuary on a 300mm lens fitted with × 2 converter. The converter allows the image to be held bigger—on the 300mm lens (with or without converter) the closest focusing distance is 4m (13ft). The 600mm lens only focuses down to 6.2m (20ft). Sometimes getting that much closer to the subject results in a more dynamic image.

On safari in Africa. There is very little colour in such locations in the middle of the day. Use a polarizer to cut reflected light and a warming filter to put some colour back into the picture. Both the safari shots, *below,* were taken on a 500mm mirror lens, fitted with a 15 Magenta filter. They were shot from a car with the camera supported on a bean bag.

There are many safari parks around the world

Be careful—even in a vehicle it can be a dangerous business. Wild animals move fast. Do not go in where you cannot get out again quickly. Unless there is a great deal of light use fast film so that the fastest shutter speeds can be used with long lenses, which, in many instances, may have to be hand held.

On an organized safari pictures can often be taken from a car window or through a wagon roof and a bean bag makes an ideal camera stand. If you do not have one, fill a carrier bag with small stones and balance it on the car window or roof. Rest the camera on the bag of stones and wait in the vehicle until a shot presents itself.

which, on quiet days, can be rewarding to visit. Clean the car windows beforehand; with the lens pressed against the glass, picture quality should not be adversely affected.

The dolphinarium act, *right*, was photographed on a 180mm lens. The final composition was the result of three previous visits to the show.

Animals

In the average city or suburban garden there is a surprising variety of wildlife. Photographing it can be as great a challenge to the animal photographer as African big game. Take any opportunity to take pictures of local wildlife and domestic creatures. Even common garden birds or a pet cat can make interesting shots.

When photographing nervous animals, as most are, think of the first shot as *the* shot. Make sure of it; the noise of the shutter will frighten the animal and it may never return. Use electronic flash when taking close-up pictures of birds to freeze them in motion.

Portable unit flashes are of such short duration that many birds do not even notice them. Those which do see the flash often get accustomed to it quickly.

To get the best results be single minded about which type of animal you wish to photograph, then determine the best location, season and time of day. Let the animal settle and never frighten it. Even small animals need room to escape.

If cornered they may panic and you could be in danger. Never get between an animal and its food.

Choose clothes to blend in with the scenery. Do not wear silvery items like belt buckles. Cover shiny equipment with black tape. Even cover yourself with camouflage netting if necessary. Carry a selection of bait, such as bread for birds and honey for insects. Binoculars are also essential for scanning the horizon when working in the country.

When shooting at a zoo or marina, find out the times for feeding or displays which often provide good opportunities for pictures. At the marina watch the show through once to look for the best viewpoint on the action.

The blue tit, *below left*, was photographed from a kitchen window. Birds are so used to activity in the house that they are not bothered by the camera shutter. Gorillas, *below*, are always a favourite attraction at the zoo. This shot was overexposed by one stop to hold detail.

A small flash unit was mounted on the camera to photograph the cat, *below right*—again overexposed to hold detail in the fur.

Use a hide when photographing shy birds or animals, such as the otter, *above*. Birds are particularly nervous of any sudden movements.

The simplest type of hide is made with four stakes knocked into the ground and covered with canvas. Leave spaces through which to shoot. Over the years nature photographers have come to realize that a hide need only be the simplest of structures. Its purpose is only to hide the photographer from the animal; it does not need to be camouflaged or made to look like a tree.

For photographing birds in their nests, the hide may have to be built up in a tree or at least high enough off the ground to see into the nest. Study the species thoroughly before investing the effort needed to set up a hide.

Once the hide has been set up it may be hours before the animal shows itself. Be prepared for a long wait—if you are lucky it will be worth it.

Travel

Successful travel photographs come from good trips and good trips come from meticulous planning. Think carefully about the equipment to take and try and pack what you are likely to need without overloading yourself. Don't buy a new camera or lens just before going away; test and be familiar with all equipment before leaving.

When away don't only look for the obvious pictures—the panoramas, the strange clothes, all the things that are different from back home. Have an eye for the more subtle, but equally interesting, details. Remember that you will show pictures to friends on your return so try and convey the atmosphere and feel of the place in your pictures. This is sometimes done more successfully with a few detail shots than with one general picture.

Shooting both colour and black and white film when travelling can be problematic; each needs a separate photographic approach. Sometimes the "human family" type of picture works better in black and white; colour can detract from the essence of the subject.

It is helpful to have a positive interest in something, rather than a "today's Monday, must be Mexico" attitude. Something that fascinates you personally may make a better picture than the city's most famous monument.

Carry a camera at all times, the compacts (see pp.16–17) are eminently portable. If you miss a good shot you will kick yourself—you won't forget the image left on your brain.

A priest and nun in a Greek island monastery were photographed in the late afternoon sun. Always ask and smile before taking such pictures and you will usually get the permission you want.

A flower seller on his barge in Srinigar, Kashmir, *preceding pages.*

Do not rush travel pictures. Although the photograph of the girl on a camel is just a snapshot it took time to get her and the camel in the right place with the best light for the picture.

● Overhead electricity cables, which appear in streets all over the world, can be a nuisance. Shoot in low light and push the film. This minimizes the unwanted lines.

● Professional photographers clean their cameras every day when they return to base. Captions can be written at the same time when the memory is fresh, and the next day's shooting schedule planned.

● Take along a Polaroid camera if for no other reason than to give pictures away. Local children begging for gifts can be a nuisance and a picture is more useful than chewing-gum.

● Most photographers shoot film in 36-exposure rolls, but film that is only used for specific types of picture (400 ISO negative, type B colour, slow black and white, for example) is more convenient in 20-exposure rolls. These can be finished in one go without having to be rewound and the cassettes marked off.

● A waist-level finder is useful for shooting people when you do not want them to react to camera. Right-angle lenses, designed for shooting around corners, can take so long to aim and focus that they become a liability, often drawing attention to the photographer.

● For many people travel is an experience shared with family and friends and it may be difficult to carry lots of camera equipment with all the other luggage to worry about. Fit the camera with an 80–200mm zoom lens for maximum flexibility, and carry other photographic items in the adapted jacket described on pp.200–1. In one of the pockets carry a 24mm lens wrapped in chamois leather and fill the other pockets with a range of accessories.

● If visiting a city for more than a few days take a "city tour" bus trip. It is a quick way of getting your bearings and discovering something about the atmosphere and layout as well as the major landmarks.

Travel

1 Spetze, Greece

2 Tuareg, Tamanrasset

3 Malindi, Kenya

Read all about a place before going there. A knowledge of local customs, main features and interesting events is helpful and doesn't detract from the excitement of first impressions.

The excitement of arriving in a new place can lead one to overshoot on the first day or try to cover too many places in a hurry. Relax, look around and take your time to get the best shots. Also, by overshooting early on you may run out of film, just when the feeling of the place has been absorbed and the film could be put to its best use.

Try choosing a location and waiting for the action to come to you. Stand back and observe before shooting a number of frames.

4 Kashmir, India

5 Istanbul, Turkey

With a 35mm lens composition has a strong curve (1) in sympathy with the shape of the boats. A 35mm lens was used (2) to "pull" in a black background. Shot (3) was taken on a Nikonos with a 35mm lens. The hard light has turned the figure into an abstract shape. A figure in a landscape is always a good subject.

People at their daily tasks (4) usually make interesting shots. Here a 180mm lens was used. A 500mm mirror lens was used to make the sun big (5), balanced to the silhouette of the mosque. At an event like (6) either shoot wide angle or look for details as here, using a 180mm lens.

Isolate pleasing pictures (7) by use of lenses. The 80–200mm zoom allows tight pictures to be composed.

6 Trooping the Colour, London

168

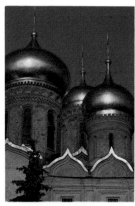

7 The Algarve, Portugal 8 Central Park, New York 9 Kremlin, Moscow

10 Shepherd, High Atlas, Morocco 11 Riviera, France

The contrast between figures and buildings **(8)** is emphasized by using a 20mm lens. Muted colour is as effective as a vibrant full colour picture. Strong sunlight picks out the golden domes **(9)** and is not affected by the polarizing filter, which has darkened only the sky. **(10)** was shot from a car on a 400mm lens, using a bean bag for support. **(11)**, shot at 3 p.m., was exposed for the intense highlight; everything else has turned dark. Always bracket in these conditions. A 105mm lens, wide open, held **(12)** "off" the background. The picture of the priest **(13)** was taken with an 80–200mm zoom in the shade, making a simple, direct composition with just enough white around the hat for emphasis

12 Kafir Kalash, Pakistan 13 Priest, Corfu

Travel

When visiting a town or city for the first time buy postcards of the places of interest. They will save you time by helping you select sights to photograph. And if there is a language barrier they can be used to show cab drivers your destination.

Once at the sight look for the camera angle the postcard photographer has chosen and try to improve on it. Then walk around and photograph the location from a variety of interesting angles with different lenses and filters.

Note the position of the sun and calculate the time when the light might be better. If necessary return to the spot to get another picture.

Don't be put off by unfavourable weather conditions; it may be possible to take a unique picture of a location that has been photographed a million times before. Find out if there are any special events or festivals taking place while you are in town.

The camera was pushed through the railings. The shadows sweep the eye into the building. Shot on a 24mm lens with polarizing and ND filters.

Try moving away from the building and using a long lens. This was shot on a 105mm lens. Out-of-focus trees that fill the sky help the composition.

If an occasion draws the crowds, get there early and make an effort to be in the right place. One often has to wait for the event to begin so do not carry too much heavy equipment. These photographs of Queen Elizabeth II's Jubilee Celebrations at Buckingham Palace were shot from the crowd. Take in the atmosphere and look for detail pictures as well as the obvious. Shoot from over the head if necessary. Photograph the people around you and their reactions to what is happening. When the event is over wait around for a while and see if there is anything of interest still to shoot.

Architecture

The effect of light on buildings is the main consideration when photographing architecture. A photographer may spend several days checking the appearance and atmosphere of a building at different times of day and in the evening when interior lights are switched on.

A change in light conditions can transform some structures. On a dull, cloudy day a building may seem flat, grey and boring, but if the clouds clear later in the afternoon, it may be bathed in golden light and appear beautiful and alive.

Buildings, like people, should be photographed in a way that brings out their individuality, their character. A sparkling, brash new building may be best taken on a sunny day with hard light picking out the steel and glass. With the help of a polarizer its uncompromising hard edges will stand out against a dramatically dark blue sky.

A Georgian terrace, on the other hand, may look at its most charming at dusk, with soft, warm, natural light and a few lamps shining in windows. An 81A filter could be used to bring this warmth to the fore. Good shots can be taken of buildings at dusk, when interior lights or external floodlights are first turned on but there is still some blue light in the sky.

CHECKPOINTS

● A compass is a great asset when photographing buildings. Calculate where the sun will be all through the day and plan for it.

● Essential accessories are a polarizing filter for colour, and orange and red filters for black and white film. Use perspective correction lenses for correcting verticals or shoot from halfway up a building opposite and avoid distortion.

● Light interiors with care—only introduce the light necessary for taking the photograph.

A perfectly symmetrical picture of St Peter's Square in Rome, *preceding pages*, was taken on a 35–70mm zoom lens for exact framing. It was shot in Kodachrome to hold all detail.

The Roman baths and Bath Abbey, *left*, were photographed on a 20mm wide angle lens. Composition was made from the air with the photographer standing in a crane bucket.

The Lloyds building in London, *right*, was shot from halfway up an adjacent building to give an unusual view. An 85mm lens was used to emphasize its structure.

An atmosphere of the modern city was achieved by using a telephoto lens to compress the highrise buildings, *below*.

Architecture

A stone mill, nestling among trees at the water's edge, was first seen in the morning when in shadow. By afternoon the scene was bathed in sunlight, creating perfect reflections and making the shot something special.

This gracious room of a Queen Anne House, *right*, was shot in daylight but with interior lights switched on. The effect of the tungsten light on daylight film creates a pleasing warmth which complements the décor.

The symmetry of the Yorkshire cottage, *below*, is emphasized by this full frame composition.

The pub interior, *below right*, was shot in daylight with no additional light. Slow film and a long exposure were used with the camera mounted on a tripod.

Sport

The 35mm camera system changed sports photography in the 1950s. The portable telelenses and motor drives enabled the photographer to get right in with the game, showing the viewer what it was like to be a player rather than just a spectator.

Sports photography has been responsible for many innovations, both in technique and camera equipment. Manufacturers see sport as a testing ground and often introduce new equipment, such as faster lenses, in time for major events.

Recent technical developments, such as wide aperture lenses, autofocus and flash sync at 1/250 second, coupled with the high image quality of fast ISO film, has made sports photography more exciting than ever before.

Good pictures are easier to achieve if the photographer knows something of the game and the particular style of play of the main participants. Don't just wait for the perfect moment to click the shutter, photograph steadily through the game; this way you are more likely to hit the button at that critical moment.

It is always interesting for the photographer to search out and photograph that ingredient which makes a champion player different from the others. Sports photography is not only concerned with freezing the moment of victory or defeat; it must also capture the spirit of endeavour and the off-court drama.

Major sports meetings are often difficult to photograph. Public seating and press enclosures are usually a long way from the action. But remember, it doesn't have to be a world class event to produce a good picture. Dramatic photographs can result from local fixtures or even from watching a bunch of enthusiastic amateurs in the park.

A gymnast working on the rings, *preceding pages,* goes through his routine quickly, so keep shooting throughout to be sure of catching a picture.

When photographing tennis or any other sport played on a set area watch the game through the viewfinder with your finger on the button to be sure of not missing a shot. Use the fast shutter programme at shutter speeds of 1/500 or 1/1000 second to catch the action.

The Welsh rugby players, *below*, were shot from a fixed camera position with a long lens and the camera mounted on a tripod. Follow action through the lens, keeping the other eye open.

The colourful sailing boats were shot from another boat, using a 300mm lens mounted on a monopod for support. The long lens allowed the photographer to stay well back, but foreshortened perspective for a dramatic, well-packed picture.

Sport

The immense physical commitment of an athlete at his peak is evident in the best sport pictures. A wide open aperture holds the subject off the background, isolating him and focusing attention on his effort. A runner sprinting toward the camera travels at about 9m (30ft) a second; it takes experience to hold sharp on a wide aperture—use autofocus if you have it.

Here, Steve Ovett responds to the roaring crowd in characteristically exultant fashion as he sweeps to victory.

When photographing motor sport try to get onto the infield where the action is happening around you. Long races with many laps allow plenty of opportunities to shoot from the same position. Pre-focus on the track. Panning shots are easiest to take on longer lenses. Shoot on slow corners if possible—the real speed is never apparent in a photograph.

Baseball in the park is a good example of a sport that can be photographed without pressure. Unlike at a major event the photographer is free to choose the best position to work from.

CHECKPOINTS

● Use the stop down button to check focus. Reload during the intervals; waste five frames rather than lose the picture because the film ran out in mid-action.

● Know the game and the players.

● Use the programme as a caption reference. Write the frame numbers on the programme for easy player identification.

● In stadiums sit in the West stand so that the late afternoon sunlight is on the East stand, not in the lens.

● Sit ten rows back in the stand to use the height rather than in the front row at a low level.

● Take pictures of people playing sport in the park: you can get much closer and it is good practice.

● Use a variety of shutter speeds, from panning at $\frac{1}{4}$ second to shooting at 1/1000 second. It may be preferable to have a little movement, such as a blurred foot or arm, in the picture rather than freezing it.

● Never chase after the peak action; anticipate where it is going to occur. Be ready and set up for the shot. It may only occur once in the day. When shooting an area such as a goalmouth or finish line with a fixed camera, tape down the lens so it does not get knocked out of focus.

● When panning with the action and using a motor drive, keep shooting while focusing for the shot.

● Autofocus is ideal for sport photography. Set the camera on continuous autofocus and shutter priority— 1/250 second or above. In theory this should give sharp, perfectly exposed pictures. Autofocus also works well when panning with the action in subdued light conditions and when the subject is coming toward you—a horse race, for example.

● Always endeavour to fill the frame with the action.

Special effects

Spectra X48 filter made by the German B + W company. This filter makes a rainbow-coloured halo of any hard spot of light—the sun in this instance. There are several types of Spectra filters which give either a prismatic slash of colour off a highlight or a more complex starburst effect such as this.

Use of double exposure. First, the girl was photographed against a white background which was overexposed by two stops on an 85mm lens. Then the lens was changed to a 24mm with a red filter and the wall was underexposed by two stops. Added together, the two exposures were correct for the picture.

Drawing with light. The girl was photographed with flash standing in a dark room against black velvet. The shutter was held open after the flash. The outline was drawn with a pencil flashlight, covered with red gelatine and held close to the girl, aiming at camera for about one minute.

Flash light is white light, but coloured light can add mood and interest to a picture. The girl was lit from the front. Another flashlight, covered with red gelatine, was then placed directly behind her head. This second flash was balanced with the front light so that they both gave the same exposure reading.

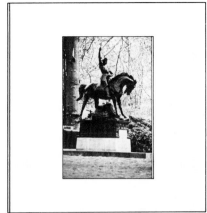

Star filter. One of the most useful of all filters, the star works on any hard spot of light. It is the obvious filter to use when photographing a Christmas tree—it makes stars of the fairy lights. The effect of this filter varies with aperture so use the preview button before shooting. Available from all filter manufacturers.

Infrared film exposed with a 60 Red filter. When using this film take incident light readings at the recommended ISO setting and bracket. In hard daylight results can be contrasty. For dramatic effect use strong filters. Experience is needed to predict the effect on the colours in the picture.

A triangular prism filter has made one daffodil look like a bunch of five. The degree of overlapping depends on how close the subject is to the camera. If the prism is rotated on a long exposure, the centre remains sharp while the outside becomes a swirl. Parallel prisms reproduce the image side by side.

The camera was set on open shutter and the lens covered until the runner moved. He was lit by a tungsten spot. A reading was taken for the highlights which gave a long exposure, so the movement would register. Two flash heads, one in front and one behind, were fired when the runner hit peak action.

Special effects

There are hundreds of filters on the market produced by many different manufacturers. All of them have a special effect on a picture, but sometimes the filter effect *is* the picture. If used too often, however, any special effect can become boring.

Anything placed in front of a high quality lens is going to affect the quality of the film image, even if only marginally. If possible, buy only the best filters made of optical glass.

Special effects need not always involve additional equipment such as filters. Interesting results can be created just by particular movements of the camera or by processing.

Graduated filter
Filters can be used to achieve a range of special effects that can make a picture. On a graduated filter colour covers only the top third of the glass, fading to clear over the rest. A magenta graduated filter was used, *right,* to add more colour to the sunset and make the picture more exotic.

Soft focus filtration
The Hasselblad Softar series 1 to 3 are the best soft focus filters on the market. Use them to add romance and glamour to a portrait. A Softar 3, used with an 81B to warm skin tones, gave a soft glow to highlights on hair and shoulders, *left.*

The effect of Softar filters varies with aperture—the wider the aperture the softer the image. Be wary of stopping down too much and reducing the effect.

Pulling zoom

Use of the full range of the zoom lens has "pulled" the lights on this pagoda into radiating streaks. To achieve this effect use a 35–105mm zoom lens and mount the camera on a tripod. If no tripod is available hold the camera as steady as possible. Using an exposure of about two seconds start shooting with the 35mm focal length, then pull the zoom through to 105mm during the second half of the exposure. Vary the speed according to the picture—the faster the movement the thinner the streaks.

Double exposure

An unusual portrait can be taken using this technique. For the first exposure the subject was positioned on the left-hand side of the frame against a black background. The camera was not wound on; a second exposure was taken on the same frame and using the same background, but with the subject moved to the right-hand side.

Special effects

Open shutter

Modern electronic flash, with durations as short as 1/15,000 second, can be used to capture a moment of movement. For the picture, *right*, the camera shutter was left open and, in semi-darkness, an olive was dropped into the glass of Martini. The flash was triggered the moment the olive hit the liquid.

With practice this works well by eye. A more sophisticated method is to target an electrical beam onto the rim of the glass. When the olive passes this it triggers the flash.

Projected image

There are several ways of using a projected image, the most common being front projection and back projection. Back projection can be used to create an exotic location in the studio. A special screen is needed which allows the image to come through. Make sure that the beam of light does not travel down the path of the lens or it will be visible.

The photograph showing an artist's impression of a black hole behind a science professor, *below*, uses front projection. An image is projected from the same side of the screen as the camera and the two images of different sizes are fitted into one picture. Be careful there are no shadows on the screen.

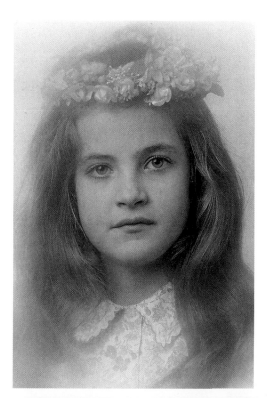

Vaseline filter

A dreamy, almost Victorian air is lent to a little girl's portrait, *left,* by this effect, which softens and diffuses the edges of the image. Using a cotton bud, apply the Vaseline to an old UV filter, leaving a clear circle, about 1cm (0.4in) in diameter, in the centre. Set a fairly wide aperture— the smaller the aperture the less the effect of the filtration. The Vaseline can also be coloured with food dye for use with colour film.

Shaped filters

These are masks which are simply placed over the lens to add somewhat gimmicky interest to a picture. Keep the lens stopped down to hold sharpness. Shapes such as keyholes, hearts and binoculars are available, or make your own from black card. A binocular filter was used, *below,* to frame the yacht.

Special effects

Heavy grain
Grain is a useful special effect for creating a painterly, impressionistic look in pictures such as portraits and landscapes. The faster the film the grainier the picture, but grain can also be achieved by duping or by processing at a higher than recommended temperature.

The girl, *above,* was photographed on Scotch 1000 with an 81C filter to give warm, glowing colours. She was flatly lit to minimize detail. The film was processed normally but a section was then copied to accentuate the grain. The result is a romantic, flattering portrait.

Using the wrong film
Type B film is designed for use indoors with tungsten light but here has been used at sunset outdoors, *above.* The strong blue cast it creates effectively disguises the ugly concrete of the building. Process as normal.

Moving lights
Use a shutter speed of 10 to 15 seconds and set aperture accordingly. The camera must be mounted on a tripod. Press the shutter just before the car appears and expose until it has gone. Only the moonlight and car lights register—red streaks for the rear lights, white for the front, *right.*

Panning

Get the subject in frame and hold him in the centre of the viewfinder as he moves, *above*. With the camera hand held, move at the same speed as the subject—he remains sharp and the background is blurred. Use an exposure of about 1/30 or 1/15 second.

Moving camera

Introduce movement into a still picture by moving the camera instead of the subject, *below*. The camera was mounted on a tripod and a long exposure used. Two thirds of the exposure were made as normal and the final third shot as the camera was moved.

Special effects

Day for night
Photography by
moonlight is not always
possible. If a night-time
shot is wanted it is
easier to shoot during
the day and make it look
like night—an effect
known as day for night.

To achieve this, use a
light blue filter (82C),
light red filter (10 Red)
and a polarizer and
expose for the
highlights. Under most
conditions this will
result in an atmospheric
night-time picture.

This Scottish
landscape was taken on
a 35mm lens with an
aperture of f11. Since the
filters increase the length
of exposure the camera
had to be mounted on a
heavy tripod.

**Orange graduated
filter**
If the sky in a black and
white picture is weak it
can be "printed in" in
the darkroom, but this is
not always successful. A
better way is to use a
graduated filter—colour
covers only the top third
of the filter, fading to
clear over the rest.

For this landscape an
orange graduated filter
was used to darken the
top third of the picture.
As a result the sky
appears more contrasty
and dramatic and the
mountains hard edged.

Using the wrong developer

If colour negative film, usually processed in C41, is E6 processed it comes out as transparency but with an interesting grainy effect.

Heavy grain can also be achieved with any film by overrating and overprocessing.

Infrared film

Black and white infrared film gives a unique semi-negative effect. It registers heat as well as light and is sensitive to wavelengths beyond the red end of the spectrum. In black and white, leaves and grass appear white and, with a 25 Red filter, blue skies become black.

Infrared is not ISO rated and can be difficult to handle. On a bright day try an exposure of 1/500 second at f8 with various strengths of red filter to deepen or lighten contrast. When focusing use the infrared (IR) setting on the lens, which compensates for the additional thickness of the film.

Infrared film must always be handled in total darkness. Load and unload in the dark.

Travel with the camera

Before starting on a trip, make sure that camera equipment and film are insured for their full replacement value. Many household policies do not cover camera equipment abroad, nor if it is left in a car.

In a hotel where security is suspect use a cycle lock to fix the handle of the (locked) camera case to the plumbing. Remember, too, that an obvious camera case might attract the attention of thieves. Some photographers conceal their camera bags inside less conspicuous luggage.

Customs

Carry several copies of lists with the serial numbers of cameras and lenses—but the value only on one. Most countries will permit the temporary import of camera equipment up to a certain value for personal use so declare the equipment to that value. The main concern of customs officials is that goods are not resold in their country. Have a list ready—it saves the officials time and looks efficient. It will be stamped and attached to your passport. Keep it safe and surrender it on your departure from the country.

Some countries subscribe to the carnet system whereby equipment of value may be imported for a limited period without attracting payment of duty. Another way of safeguarding against payment of duty is to arrange with a home bank to lodge a bond covering the amount of duty on the cameras in the main bank of the country being visited. Cancel the bond on return.

The traveller with one camera and two or three lenses seldom has difficulties with customs, but some professionals have spent weeks trying to retrieve impounded cameras. Avoid such problems by carrying the right papers.

If cameras are bought abroad keep all the paperwork. Even if equipment was bought at home, carry receipts for everything to show on your return. The customs know by the serial number on the camera whether the batch was officially imported.

The number of cameras and lenses and amount of film that can be imported varies from country to country. Check with a travel agency or with the embassy of the country concerned before travelling with equipment.

All these problems will be eased within the EEC (European Economic Community) in 1992, when customs and border regulations are to be relaxed.

Establish a method of captioning pictures and recording exposure details. There is no perfect way, but having a good memory helps.

Tape onto the back of the camera a piece of paper folded lengthways into four; this gives one side per film for eight films. Write a brief description of the shot and exposure details next to the frame numbers. Later, transcribe the information to a master caption book containing other background information. This is a good method to use if there are a lot of difficult names to spell or if several cameras are being used. For electronic cameras multi-control backs are available that print data such as date, time and frame number on the film.

The photographer's record sheet, *above*, was styled for use in personal organizers. It has separate columns for film number, type of film and filter used, description of the shot, exposure and processing.

Packing

Good pictures come from efficient preparation, which starts with packing. Empty the camera bag and start again from scratch so you know what is there and where it is. Check that items such as tripod screws, flash leads, filters and spare batteries have been included.

Pack the camera with the shutters uncocked so there is no strain on the shutter spring. Set lenses on the widest aperture so there is no strain on the iris and check that nothing is pressing down on levers. These measures do not apply to electronic cameras, which have no mechanical functions. Make sure that any spare batteries are not in contact with metal objects.

Cameras are likely to be subjected to bumps, knocks and vibration during travel, none of which does a precision instrument any good. Check that the corners of the camera case are well padded to give as much protection as possible.

Wrong

Correct

Hold the camera in the palm of the right hand with index finger on the trigger. Left hand supports and maintains focus. Use the right eye; this leaves room to wind on without moving the camera. Use the camera as if shooting a rifle. Make yourself stable, keep elbows in, feet apart. Squeeze the trigger; do not jerk it.

Wrong   Correct

Film

Remove film from the camera when crossing politically sensitive borders; an official may open the camera causing damage to loaded film.

If you run out of film abroad, check that the film you buy is in date. Try and buy from a shop that has a large turnover. "Process paid" film can be processed in a country other than the one where it was bought—as long as there is a plant there. But don't take the risk of expecting the processor to mail the film back to the home country. Don't post Kodachrome home in the yellow envelopes: it could be stolen and resold as fresh film. Mail the film in plain envelopes, enclosing the yellow envelopes as a sign that process costs have been paid.

The cost of film varies from country to country. In some countries it is so valuable that photographers have used it as currency. If possible take what you need with you, or buy from a respectable dealer or duty free shop.

X-ray machines at many airports carry signs which claim that they do not damage film. However, if the machine is at full power there is a great risk to film although the effects may not be immediately obvious. Colour transparency and black and white film may take on a hazy, milky quality, for example. Be safe and ask for a hand check, especially if carrying film rated above 1000 ISO.

Adverse conditions

Cameras need constant loving care and daily attention when they are being used in adverse conditions.

Extreme cold

If a camera is to be used in temperatures below − 45°C (− 49°F) the oil should be changed for one of a much finer grade. The normal camera oil congeals at sub-zero temperatures, rendering the camera useless. Once a camera has been winterized, do not use it in normal temperatures; this would cause excessive wear.

Carry camera equipment in a hermetically sealed metal case. Leather, canvas and rubber lose their natural properties when they freeze. Cold canvas, for example, snaps like a piece of thin wood. Gaffer tape can be used to seal equipment against fine snow, but is only effective down to temperatures of − 10°C (14°F). Take great care when touching metal parts, especially with the face. Skin can stick to the frozen metal and be torn off— an extremely painful wound which takes a long time to heal.

Try to keep cameras at a constant temperature; bringing them into a warm room from the cold causes condensation to form inside the camera body. The moisture then freezes on contact with the outside air. Put cameras in airtight plastic bags containing packets of silica gel before bringing them indoors. The condensation will then form on the outside of the bag and not in the cameras.

Cameras worn under an anorak are protected from the weather. But if you start perspiring, the moisture soon freezes on the camera. Snow landing on a camera that is warmer than the outside temperature melts and immediately freezes again. Wind-blown snow can be as fine as talcum powder, so make sure all hinges, cracks and joints are sealed.

Keep film as cool as the camera. Do not subject it to great changes in temperature; this can upset the colour balance. In adverse conditions it is generally best to use amateur E6 colour film rather than professional—amateur film has been manufactured for a longer shelf life and is more stable. Cold "freeze dries" film making it brittle, so do not wind on too quickly or the sprocket holes may tear. Wind manually in extreme cold: the sudden movement of a winder can rip film that is under stress. Cold film can be razor sharp so handle carefully.

The light in polar regions causes several exposure problems. In summer it is very bright and clean, but for many weeks there is no direct light. Exposures in cold regions can vary from 1/500 second at f8 with 25 ISO film on one day, to 1/125 second at f4 with 400 ISO film the next. Take every speed of film.

In mountainous regions the light can be so bright it almost goes off the meter scale. Use polarizing and graduated filters to put some form and shape back into areas of snow which are reflecting the light. Keep battery-powered meters inside your jacket and only bring them out when needed. The Luna Six works well in extreme cold.

Humid tropics

High humidity is the major problem in tropical conditions. Going between air-conditioned buildings and the humid air outside causes glass to fog over and takes a long time to clear. Keep equipment constantly outside rather than in if possible.

In damp heat fungus grows on film and leather, stitching rots and rubber splits. Tiny creatures may even take up residence in cameras. If there is not an electric dehumidifier available, keep camera and film in sealed plastic bags with several packets of silica gel; carry the bags in a hermetically sealed camera case. Do not open rolls of film until needed; seal exposed rolls in plastic containers, also with a bag of silica gel. Dry the gel out periodically by putting it into a domestic oven for a few minutes.

Desert

Ground temperatures in the desert can be more than 50°C (122°F). If cameras are left unprotected in such heat they become untouchable. Direct sun on a camera may melt the cement and glue holding the lens elements in place, causing them to shift if the camera is jolted. When the lens cools down again the materials contract at different rates, which can cause permanent damage.

Keep cameras in silver-coloured cases to reflect the sun or make a foil covering for a soft bag. Don't place any case on the ground or on a car roof—allow air to circulate around it.

Clean and maintain equipment at night when it is cool. Store film in a metal case with a thick polystyrene inner case which is only opened at night. It will remain relatively cool all day. A camera wrapped in chamois leather at night will stay cool well into the day.

A plastic bag protects the camera from rain, snow, or dust. Cut a hole for the lens and secure it with tape. Keep right hand in the bag, left one outside.

Dust

Electronic cameras such as the F-801 are well sealed and should resist dust. Older cameras are not sealed units. Give some protection from dust by applying Vaseline or Nikonos "O" ring grease around the joints of the meter head, lens mount, hinges and grooves at the back. The dust gets trapped in the grease. Tape over all exterior parts which are not in use such as the flash sync, motor drive terminals, battery check button, and levers. Never apply any form of grease to electronic cameras.

The strong moulded plastic Pelican case is ideal for use in the harshest conditions. It is waterproof, dustproof, insulated against cold and heat, and floats on water.

Sea water

Salt water and even salty sea air can cause permanent damage by corroding the metal parts of a camera. The best protection against sea water damage is to insure the camera; if it falls in, claim for a new one as nothing much can be done to repair it.

If a camera is exposed to spray, wipe the metalwork periodically with a swab of lint lightly soaked in WD40. Keep it off the lens and apply sparingly. The use of toughened plastics in most modern cameras has reduced the amount of metal and they are less at risk from corrosion.

An inflated inner tube provides much needed stability when shooting from a low angle in the water. The elbows are supported, leaving the hands free to work camera controls. The head is kept higher out of the water than with a life jacket alone.

Clothing □ I

The ideal jacket is comfortable, keeps you warm and dry and has plenty of pockets for carrying equipment. The lightweight U.S. Army combat jacket, *right*, is perfect and there are now custom-made photographers' jackets with similar features. All are of light, natural fibre and have deep side pockets and inside pockets that can be securely fastened. A hood folded into the collar is a useful feature and also gives good support for the camera strap around your neck. A standard safari or bush jacket is also suitable, but is more expensive and may be too tailored.

Whatever type of jacket is chosen, make sure it is loose fitting and avoid manmade fibres. All pockets should be secure. Velcro tabs are excellent—they are quick to use and noisy, which may discourage pickpockets.

Extra pockets can be added on the sleeves. This may sound an unlikely place for a pocket, but it is easily accessible and the bulk doesn't get in the way. Inside pockets should be deep. Put a handkerchief and a chamois leather in with small things to stop them bouncing out.

Keep all official passes handy. If called upon to show a pass it is more impressive to find it first time rather than search around for ages. Some people wear trousers with pockets on the thighs for documentation and maps.

Jeans are fine, unless conditions are wet and cold—then they are uncomfortable. Trousers should be strong, since time may well be spent kneeling or even lying on wet or rocky ground. The knees always seem to go first.

Avoid military-style clothing in politically sensitive countries. Some people associate cameras with spies, so look like a tourist. Officials, armed or unarmed, are the same the world over: they are suspicious of photographers. So if you really want an official to be on your side and to do a favour for you, don't dress outrageously and try to give a good impression. Remember, it is the picture that counts.

Wear cotton shirts with high collars, so camera straps don't cut into the neck, and good breast pockets for money, passport and other important items. Wear a money belt around the waist if you feel really threatened.

A few other tips learned from bitter experience. It is better to have things in separate pockets than everything jumbled up in one. Really long hair can get tangled in camera straps or in the way of the lens. Photographers tend to be on their feet most of the time so make sure footwear is sound, comfortable and well broken in. Wear wool socks in most climates and cotton in the heat. Nylon socks can cause blisters and aching feet.

The Banana Republic waistcoat is loose fitting and comfortable for hot climates, where a jacket would be too warm. It has eight well-distributed pockets, with ample room for all the items on the opposite page. There is also an additional pocket on the back of the waistcoat in which a lightweight anorak can be carried in case of rain.

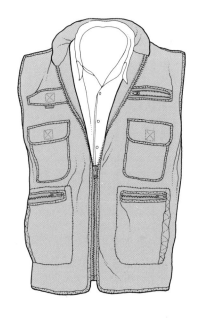

A pad of good quality lens tissues. Maps, postcards, copies of relevant reference materials. Pocket tape recorder and spare tape.

Hard bristle brush and soft sable brush. Compass. Meter with spot attachment (wear strap around the neck).

Sunglasses, which can be used as polarizing filter. Passes, credentials, letters of accreditation.

Unexposed film in cans—one type to a pocket. Write identification on cans.

Shot film—numbered on cans.

Notebook, fine pen, thick indelible pen.

Swiss army knife.

Front/back lens caps, body cap, piece of chamois leather.

The most used filters: 1 or 2 polarizing filters, 81, ND and graduated.

Clothing ☐ 2

When setting out to take pictures in cold or wet weather always dress for warmth and comfort. You will work all the better for it. Bear in mind when shooting outdoors that long periods may be spent waiting for the right moment, so be prepared. Respect nature, it always has the upper hand.

A parka is a good all-weather garment, but always carry a three-quarter length windproof jacket (or *cagoule*), too. A cold wind can be lethal. When the chill factor is taken into account the temperature may be more than ten degrees lower than indicated.

Zip cameras up inside the jacket to keep them warm and dry. Keep the batteries warm. With some cameras it is possible to keep the motor drive battery pack in a pocket with a short cable connecting it to the camera.

Never carry too much equipment. Energy is needed to keep warm. In wet, dew, hill fog or condensation, keep the camera parts in plastic bags and off the ground.

Genuine Harris Tweed trousers give excellent protection in wet or cold. They are always warm and the material dries quickly in the wind. Specialist climbing stores now offer many types of light thermal clothing for keeping out the cold. Keep waterproof footwear and a large golf umbrella in the car at all times.

A good coat is the first line of defence against bad weather. The layers under-

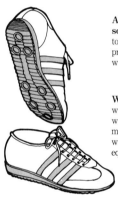

A fisherman's sou'wester worn back to front gives good protection in the rain when using short lenses.

Wear training shoes with non-slip soles if weather permits. You must be sure-footed when carrying equipment.

Bumbag

Carry a lightweight showerproof anorak. Useful for protecting both camera and photographer in a sudden shower.

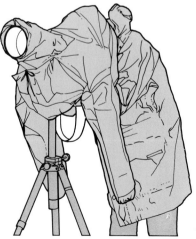

An extra anorak can be used to cover a camera mounted on the tripod. Carry one small enough to pack into the belt of a ski "bumbag". Folded, the anorak also makes a good ground sheet.

neath keep you warm as long as the coat is made of strong, tightly woven fabric to keep out the wind and rain. The Berghaus/Gore-tex coat, *below*, is an excellent example. Windproof and waterproof, it keeps the wearer warm but allows the body to breathe. Coat zips should have Velcro seals to stop the zip freezing. The hood should have wire around the face area so you can bend the opening into a slit and get maximum protection.

In extreme dry cold wear a goose down suit, *below right*, with a windproof Berghaus/Gore-tex coat over the top.

Thermal underwear   **Fibre-pile suit**

A wool balaclava does not impede vision and can be rolled up into a hat.

Thermal underwear, *top left*, designed for climbing, allows perspiration to pass through to the next layer of clothing.

The Helly Hanson or North Cape fibre-pile suit with hood and jacket, *top right*. The cuffs hook round the thumb, keeping the wrist warm.

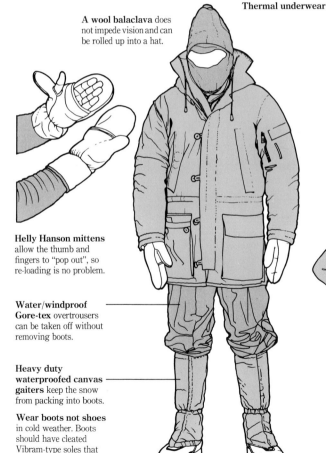

Helly Hanson mittens allow the thumb and fingers to "pop out", so re-loading is no problem.

Water/windproof Gore-tex overtrousers can be taken off without removing boots.

Heavy duty waterproofed canvas gaiters keep the snow from packing into boots.

Wear boots not shoes in cold weather. Boots should have cleated Vibram-type soles that give good footing on most surfaces.

Duvet jacket. Goose down is light and extremely warm as long as it is kept dry, but is useless if wet. Wear under a waterproof Gore-tex coat.

Travel □ medical

Before setting out for an exotic location take the latest medical advice and check all vaccinations are up to date. Arrange adequate insurance and make sure it pays for you and your family to be flown home in an emergency.

If travelling to hot countries or high altitudes take precautions against sunburn and sunstroke. Carry sunhats, sunglasses and high factor protective creams.

When travelling by plane eat small, light meals and drink plenty of water to combat dehydration. Don't drink too much alcohol. Take aspirin, toothbrush, lip salve and moisturizing cream.

Take precautions against the following diseases whether or not vaccination is a condition of entry to a country:

A first aid box should include: eye ointment and drops, bandages, antibiotics, water purifying tablets, glucose and salt, aspirin, travel sickness pills, antihistamines, sticking plaster, insect repellent, needle, iodine, alcohol and scissors.

Tetanus is caused by contamination of wounds. A course of three injections is spread over a period of at least twelve weeks.

Yellow fever is transmitted by mosquitoes. An International Certificate of vaccination is required by many countries.

Typhoid and cholera are contracted from contaminated water or food. Vaccination is advisable, and may be insisted upon, when travelling to countries where these diseases are common.

Poliomyelitis. If unvaccinated, a full course of three injections is necessary. People vaccinated more than ten years ago need a booster dose before travelling to high-risk areas.

Hepatitis is a viral liver infection. If travelling to Third World countries or any other areas where this is common have gamma globulin injections, which reduce the severity of any subsequent infection.

Malaria is transmitted by mosquito bites. It can usually be prevented by taking anti-malarial pills for as long as the instructions state—before departure, while in a malarial zone and, most importantly, after returning home. Insect repellent, mosquito nets and protective clothing help prevent mosquito bites.

AIDS is transmitted by sexual intercourse, use of infected needles and transfusion with infected blood. Some travellers to high-risk areas now carry kits containing disposable hypodermic needles in case injections are needed. Know your blood group.

Photographers working in extreme climates should be aware of the following conditions:

Heat stroke. In hot climates the body loses fluids quickly and the need for water is greatly increased. Since salt is lost in the sweat, prolonged sweating can lead to salt depletion and cramps. In extreme heat and high humidity, the body temperature rises; above 40°C (105°F) collapse can occur.

Drink lots of water with a teaspoonful of salt per pint. If you begin to feel the adverse effects of the heat, rest in the shade and sponge the body down every ten minutes.

Frostbite usually affects extremities such as toes, nose, ears and fingertips. The onset can be insidious and almost painless. The first sign of frostnip, the early stage, is usually a tingling sensation. The area goes white and needs to be massaged or rubbed to get the circulation going.

Travel □ legal

In Iceland a permit is required to photograph nesting birds. In Jamaica the authorities disapprove of people who photograph beggars. In some Third World countries the main civil airports are also military bases where the strictest security regulations apply. Offenders who are ignorant of such local laws may lose the film in their camera and even their freedom. Ask the advice of the embassy before visiting an area known to be politically sensitive.

In most Western countries there are no restrictions on taking pictures in public places. In Britain the 1988 Copyright, Designs and Patents Act introduced a limited right of privacy. Where photographs are commissioned for private use the person commissioning the work has the right not to have the work published or shown publicly, even though, in most cases, copyright will vest in the photographer. Other countries have more extensive privacy laws, and in some, such as the United States, France and West Germany, a person's image cannot be used for merchandising without their consent. If a photograph is used which suggests that a person endorses a product he or she may have grounds to file suit against the photographer. In France a householder's privacy is invaded if a picture of the house is used without permission.

A model release form signed by the subject, and specifically including a waiver of the subject's right of privacy, is the photographer's protection. This should cover all eventualities such as the finished print being retouched or incorporated into a collage.

The more comprehensive the release form the less chance the model will have to sue the photographer. Whenever a paid model is used a contract should be drawn up which includes a section whereby they waive all rights to the picture.

Pictures of people in public places can be used for most artistic or editorial purposes, but in some countries the subject's consent is required if the picture is to be used for merchandising purposes.

Very "indiscreet" pictures run the risk of libel claims. Events that are newsworthy are generally considered to be public property; so too are the images of celebrities such as film stars, who normally court publicity.

Pictures shot in private places such as theatres, sports arenas and private houses are a different matter. Under local bylaws or conditions of entry a person taking photographs may be guilty of trespass and in some places equipment can be confiscated. In most British art galleries photography is not permitted; some European and American galleries do allow pictures for personal use only to be taken.

The procedure for purchasing and publishing photographs varies from company to company. Some contracts involve signing away all rights to a picture, which then becomes the property of the buyer. Think carefully before selling photographs this way. Professionals don't do it unless paid a great deal of money.

Other publishers have more reasonable agreements by which they purchase the rights to use a picture. If there is a repeat use in another context or country the photographer may receive a further fee.

The photographer generally retains copyright on his pictures, unless he has signed it away. But if the photographer is an employee and takes the pictures in the course of his employment copyright will vest in the employer. Read contracts carefully. The copyright laws are confusing and in many countries are being revised in favour of the photographer.

Work should never be submitted to an agency or publisher without a delivery note with terms clearly stated. Draft contracts are available from the national unions that represent photographers. Fees for use and penalties for loss, damage or delayed return should be stated. Without the client's signature the photographer will have no grounds for making any claims.

Faults on film

Sometimes a roll of film which comes back from processing includes pictures which do not look at all like the ones you remember taking. The faults discussed here are common to all cameras and all types of colour and black and white film. Even the most seasoned professionals make mistakes occasionally, but with a careful and methodical approach these faults can usually be avoided.

The photographer must be familiar with his equipment, but not to the point of contempt. The shots which are ruined are too often those you most want.

Hair can get into the back of the camera and lodge in the track in which the shutter runs. A similar, less sharp image appears if a hair is caught on the back of the lens. Check both areas when reloading film.

Unsynchronized flash occurs when too fast a shutter speed is used—usually more than 1/250 second. Check that the shutter speed dial is not accidentally moved during use. Most modern SLR cameras sync at 1/60 or slower with all types of flash.

Shutter bounce is caused by a slack spring on the shutter. The trailing curtain bounces back instead of closing the shutter opening, allowing a fraction more light onto the film. An easy fault for a dealer to repair.

Fogging is what happens to the film if the back of the camera is opened. Wind film back after exposure. If the back is opened, five or six frames are usually lost. Tape the back shut if it is likely to pop open accidentally.

Double exposure. Even with several bodies it is sometimes necessary to change films in mid-roll. To avoid double exposures, write the number of shot frames on the leader of partly exposed film.

Motor drive fault 1. After loading a motor drive camera and winding on, it is usual to reset the film counter. This shot is a result of not setting the dial correctly and winding on too much to begin with. The motor fired twice.

Motor drive fault 2. The motor drive dial was set on 1/60 second, but the actual shutter speed required and set on the camera was ¼ second. The result is that the film is transported during the exposure making highlights streak.

Raindrops on a lens act like small lenses and distort the picture. They are most noticeable on wide angles as individual drops, but on longer lenses they appear as blurs. Use a UV or 1A filter and a big lens hood in the rain.

Vignette is a rounding of the frame corners caused by using the wrong lens hood or fitting too many filters. Bellows can also cause vignetting if they are extended too far. Check with the preview button, looking at a light area.

Flare. A hard light shining directly into the lens can either project the shape of the aperture opening, *left*, or create rings of light and loss of colour by overexposure. Wide aperture telephoto lenses are most susceptible and may need a French flag to mask light.

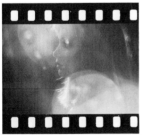

If exposed film is black it may not have been loaded properly and has not gone through the camera.

Another cause of this fault can be that the shutter is not in sync with the aperture of the camera and no light is hitting the film.

If exposed film is white but with black lines between frames, too much light has reached it. The shutter is staying open too long and is faulty or the aperture is not stopping down.

207

Processing and printing

Unless a photographer is deeply involved in photographic chemistry there is little point in trying to develop colour transparency film. The best way to get consistently good results is to build up a friendly relationship with a local laboratory. Use a professional laboratory if possible—it is worth waiting a day or so to get important pictures processed well.

If in doubt as to which laboratory to choose, ask professionals where they get their processing done.

Learn the terminology to avoid being talked down to by laboratory assistants. Good small laboratories are often willing to take time to discuss the results and an amateur can get good advice from them.

All films that use the E6 process have the advantage that their effective film speed can be altered by changing the time in the first development bath. To double the film's speed (known as pushing one stop) the first developing process is run for an extra two minutes. Film can be pushed by stages of one half stop, or even by a third of a stop, in labs that give a personal service.

It is also possible to "pull" films by cutting the development time by two minutes per stop. This effectively reduces the film speed.

The more a film is pushed the greater will be its contrast and the coarser the grain. Conversely, pulling the film reduces contrast and flattens the image. In a laboratory an underexposed transparency is called "thick" and an overexposed one "thin".

The greater attention to agitation in hand processing makes it usually preferable to machine work. Constant agitation of the chemicals gives brighter, cleaner colour.

High speed Ektachrome films can easily be pushed two or even three stops if a grainy effect is wanted or if the exposure has been made in low light.

Kodachrome, too, can now be pushed

CHECKPOINTS

● Pushing E6 films warms the colour. Cutting by more than one and a half stops makes whites go bluish. Some laboratories produce warmer results than others.

● Take a clip test (two or three frames off the front of the roll) and calculate the amount of push or cut required to balance the colour. Send the remaining film back immediately. Colour balance of chemicals may alter overnight or over a weekend when the laboratories are not in action.

● Black and white processing is simple. It requires little equipment but lots of care. The effective speed of all black and white films can be altered by changing the development time. The contrast is also affected by development time, temperature of developer and the amount of agitation. But whether processing your own film or using a lab, there is no point pushing up the speed—and the grain and contrast—of a slow film if a faster film can be used for the picture in the first place.

● There are many different developers on the market. A few of the most useful are: Ilford Hyfen for the sharpest results and fine grain on slow films; Agfa Rodinal for high quality at any speed—this is a one-shot developer thrown away after use; Aculux for the best possible grainy effect; Acuspecial for best results with high speed film. New T-Max developers are good for other films as well as T-Max; a critical exacting chemical.

● Processing colour negative film is not complicated but requires greater attention to time and temperature control than black and white film. Half the fun of negative film is that the user can do his or her own processing and printing and so exercise greater control over the final prints.

or pulled. In the United States Kodachrome no longer has to be processed by Kodak and can be taken to independent laboratories. Elsewhere it must be processed by Kodak or one of their agents. Kodak is excellent film to use when processing cannot be done for a long time after exposure.

Colour prints

Anyone with a darkroom equipped to handle black and white and an enlarger with a filter slide can make Cibachrome colour prints from transparencies. The process is simple, the quality excellent, and the printer has absolute control. The Cibachrome image is permanent and, since it is printed onto plastic paper, tough. It is also remarkably cheap.

It is better to print from a transparency, which can be seen, rather than use a negative, which demands that the print be matched to a memory of the colour. The photographer can control the colour balance on the camera and produce the desired result. This is then the perfect guide for the print and, if necessary, the colour balance can be corrected. If the print is being made at a laboratory they can refer to the transparency when making the print.

By shooting colour negative and making your own prints it is possible to achieve effects that would otherwise involve far too difficult a brief for a laboratory. Colour printing is based on the principle of adding and subtracting complementary filters. Total familiarity with this principle and the practices involved is essential for good results.

Printing houses can provide good, cheap, machine-made prints from average quality negatives or transparencies, but they must be thoroughly briefed. If the print is to be made from a difficult original, order one larger than 25cm × 20cm (10in × 8in)—larger formats are too big for the machines and the printer has to control the process personally.

R-types are taken directly from the original, without an internegative. They

Kodachrome is mounted by machine. An electric eye uses the black line between the frames as a guide to cut the film.

If a picture has a strong overall black background with an offcentre image, there is a danger that the machine may centre the image in the wrong place. Farther into the roll, pictures may be mounted with the frame line running down the middle. To avoid this happening, cut the right-hand corner by the address panel on the yellow prepaid envelope provided with the film and the film will be returned in one long roll.

are cheap but can also be of high quality.

The Kodak C-type system of internegatives is one of the best for quality. A negative is made from the transparency, then printed as normal.

Cheap prints can be made from a transparency or print in a few moments on a colour Xerox machine. The quality is not photographic—the prints have the appearance of a printed page. Although Xerox prints do not have the contrast or strength of colour of Ciba or Kodak prints they are well worth experimenting with and useful for getting an idea of how pictures might look.

Equally fast but better quality copies of colour prints can be obtained from a colour laser copier. The machine scans the original five times—once for balance and once for each colour (magenta, cyan, yellow and black)—and produces the copy in a matter of seconds. Colours can be strengthened or taken back.

Originals can be enlarged from 50 to 400 percent and can be printed in any single colour; the machine can also be programmed to change any colour to another.

A film scanner, linked to the copier, enables copies of 35mm transparencies and negatives to be made.

Retouching

Always keep developing and print work spotlessly clean. The importance of this becomes apparent when prints reveal spots, water marks, hairs or scratches which can ruin their appearance.

These blemishes are almost always on the film (whether negative or transparency) and when seen on the final print are greatly magnified. The size of a 35mm frame limits the amount of retouch work that can be done on the film, so the blemishes are usually treated on the print itself.

There is also a creative aspect to retouching which elevates the craft to the level of art form. Most of the dynamic photographic advertisements in magazines and on billboards have been heavily retouched, either to add emphasis to certain features or to eliminate less desirable characteristics. Many of these shots are actually composite pictures with joins skilfully blended in by the retoucher. Glamour portraits and publicity shots are also often retouched to banish imperfections from the subject.

Another aspect of the retoucher's work has been seen from time to time in news pictures from totalitarian countries. Once prominent figures have mysteriously disappeared from photographs by the hand of the censor's retoucher. No photographer should condone such alterations on pictures.

Although artistic expertise is vital to some aspects of photographic retouching, the process of "spotting" a print is comparatively simple. Careful attention to detail and a firm hand are all that are needed. Black spots on white areas of a print are usually from pin holes in the negative. These are best removed by gentle scraping with a scalpel blade or by bleaching. White spots are the result of dust or dirt on the negative and these can be painted out with a matching tone of photo dye.

Sometimes the overall effect of a picture can be enhanced by cleaning up unnecessary detail which detracts from the composition.

The photograph, *top right*, was cleaned and retouched to achieve a finished print, *bottom right*, using the following techniques:

1 White out background to give prominence to the subject. Mask with low-tack transparent masking film. Cut the film on the print—it takes practice to get the right pressure without cutting the print. Bleach with dilute potassium ferricyanide applied with a cotton swab. This process can be used to lighten the background as well as white it out.

2 Soften edges to avoid a hard outline to the head. Use permanent white gouache mixed with sepia watercolour to warm the tone. Apply with a fine brush.

3 Hair and fluff in the enlarger leave white marks. "Spot" them out with diluted photo dye. Use a small brush.

4 Black marks are from scratches on the negative. Remove them with a scalpel blade. Use it gently—only scrape off the top layer of paper. Experience is needed to judge the necessary pressure. If you do scratch too far, tone the white paper with photo dye.

5 Remove chemical stains with sepia/white/lamp-black mix. Apply with an air brush to get an even, continuous coverage.

Achieve an even tone with an air brush. These are expensive pieces of equipment, usually run off compressors. To save on initial outlay, use a foot pump or aerosol pressure pack. Alternatively, an inflated innertube will hold enough air for all but prolonged usage.

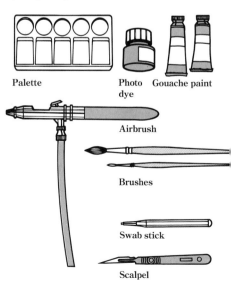

Palette

Photo dye   Gouache paint

Airbrush

Brushes

Swab stick

Scalpel

1
2
3
4
5

211

Filing and viewing

Devise an orderly filing system for negatives and transparencies so that you can always find pictures easily. Feed new pictures into the system as soon as they are processed.

Number all the negative bags, keeping each film in a separate bag, and enter the numbers in a notebook. Add brief descriptions of the shots on each roll of film.

Write as much information as you have on the bag and make a contact sheet of each film. Write the film number on the back of the paper before processing. A 36-exposure roll fits onto 25cm × 20cm (10in × 8in) paper if the film is cut into strips of five or six frames. File the negatives away consecutively in boxes or files and keep the contacts separately in another file. The contacts are then available for easy reference. Do not allow the master file of contacts out of the house or studio at any time.

There are many designs of negative bag on the market. One of the best is a clear acetate divided sheet which takes a complete film in strips and has a caption panel at the top. The film can be contacted while in the sleeve and filed on a hanger in a filing cabinet. This type of sheet is often used in the darkrooms of magazine publishers where speed and efficiency are essential.

This system is particularly useful if space is limited, but it is still advisable to keep contacts in a separate file, for two reasons.

First, it takes an experienced picture editor or darkroom printer to read negatives; second, as any professional photographer will attest, it is useful to be able to look through the old contact file occasionally—you may discover good shots that had been previously overlooked. A picture taken years ago, which seemed insignificant at the time, may acquire a

A plastic moulded seed tray makes a good box for storing edited slides.

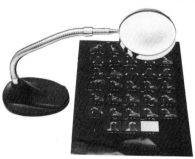

Keep negatives dry. Do not pack drawers too tightly. The negative notebook should contain all the details on the neg bag.

Several types of contact viewer are available. The flexible-arm model is useful when retouching.

new importance in years to come.

The best files for transparencies are the plastic sheets with pockets for holding 24 or 20 individual slides. There are two types. One has punch holes on the side for filing in a ring binder. The other has a large protective flap covering the front and a strip at the top which allows it to be hung directly in a filing cabinet. Such sleeves allow easy viewing of slides in series and provide quick access to the best shots. Keep rejects in boxes and, as with contacts, look at them occasionally. There will often be one or two pictures which, on a second look, seem worth rescuing from obscurity.

Viewing transparencies

A light box is essential equipment for viewing transparencies. There are many excellent makes on the market at a range of prices; but it is possible to construct a simple one for yourself, using opaque glass or white acrylic sheet and daylight fluorescent tubes.

A cheap light box, however, does not give a sufficiently accurate light for colour judgement. Transparencies for reproduction should be viewed on a printer's light box, which provides controlled illumination. The light tubes are monitored and replaced after a fixed period.

Use an eyeglass lens to view transparencies on the light box, although ready-mounted slides can be viewed on battery or electric-powered hand viewers. One of the best examples of this type of viewer is the Agfascop 100.

The best lens for viewing transparencies is the Schneider magnifier. This high-quality lens allows the full 35mm frame to be viewed. There are many other types of viewer now available, but most let top light through onto the transparency which diffuses the image.

When transparencies are returned from the processor, put them in the box the right way up. Draw diagonal lines across the top as a guide to restacking them.

A transparency light box should be fitted with colour corrected fluorescent tubes. These give an even, overall light and do not overheat. The Schneider 4X wide angle loupe covers the whole 35mm frame. The Agfascop viewer is an essential aid to selecting slides.

Put the selected slides into acetate covers, file them in plastic holders and hang in a cabinet.

Consecutive numbering stamps are useful for giving each slide the same number as the one in the notebook. Have another stamp to identify the slides with the photographer's name.

Projectors

The very best way to see and appreciate photographs is as large, high-quality reproductions in a well-printed magazine or book. Next best is to view them well projected on a large screen in a darkened room.

A transparency may look insignificant on a light box, but when projected and seen large it becomes much more interesting. Detail and close-up shots usually look more dramatic when projected.

A slide does not begin to discolour until it has been projected many times. Do not project favourite pictures for too long in a projector without a built-in cooling system: they might melt before your eyes—an interesting but distressing experience.

Black and white prints copied onto Kodachrome take on a slight blue cast, which adds to the quality of the projected image.

The best sort of screen to project on is one that gives an even reflection all over, not just on the light path where a hot spot is created. Modern super white emulsion paints have a reflective ingredient in them and are suitable for painting an interior wall for use as a screen. Conventional screens have a dark border; this could be painted onto the wall to help contain the projected image.

The Kodak Carousel has not altered in its basic design for many years. This projector is one of the most popular for audio-visual programmes, some of which run continuously for many days. The Carousel is also used for large studio back projections, and has a cooling unit attached to prevent the slides from melting.

Most major magazines, advertising agencies, conference centres, schools and institutions use Carousels. The projector is supplied with a remote control unit which controls the focus and picture change—both forward and backward.

The Carousel magazine can only be changed while the machine is switched on. Turn the counter to 0 before attempting to remove it. Make sure the spring clip is in place at all times.

Kodak CAROUSEL S-AV 2050 AF projector

Kodak Carousel

Back projection unit/light box

DIASTAR 350

WOTAN

There is a range of lenses to choose from. Carousels are available worldwide and can be run off all types of electricity supply.

The Carousel tray holds 80 or 140 slides. To empty the tray of pictures, turn it upside down, allowing the slides to fall into the lid. With a slight twist, open it and run a finger around the tray, stacking the slides into blocks. This is much easier than taking all the slides out individually.

The Kodak stack loader is a projection unit similar to the Carousel but with automatic focus. It will take the circular Carousel tray, as well as the stack loading magazine. The slides are put into the leader as a block, making it useful for editing material straight from the laboratory. This model is only made to run off 110V electricity.

The Leitz Pradovit projector has a similar design to that used by Rollei, Agfa and several other manufacturers. They use trays that hold either 36 or 50 transparencies. The trays are cheap and are good to use for storing slides when not in use.

Back projection units are loaded with the slides the right way up and the emulsion facing the screen—the opposite way to a conventional projector. As with the Leitz, the transparencies are fed into the projector in straight trays.

This type of unit is useful when editing transparencies and for tabletop presentations since the viewing room does not have to be blacked out. As with all back projection units the texture of the fresnel screen is visible when viewed from an angle.

Size of lens and distance between projector and screen image needed to achieve approximate width of screen image

Width of screen image:	1.02m	1.27m	1.52m	1.83m	2.44m	3.05m	3.66m
	40ins	50ins	60ins	72ins	96ins	120ins	144ins

Focal length of lens:	m.	ft.	m.	ft.	m.	ft.	m.	ft.	m.	ft.	m.	ft.	m.	ft.
	Distance between screen and projector to give above screen sizes													
60mm	1.83	(6)	2.13	(7)	2.9	(9½)	3.2	(10½)	4.27	(14)	5.33	(17½)	6.4	(21)
85mm	2.59	(8½)	3.2	(10½)	3.96	(13)	4.57	(15)	6.1	(20)	7.62	(25)	9.14	(30)
100mm	3.05	(10)	3.8	(12½)	4.57	(15)	5.49	(18)	7.16	(23½)	9.14	(30)	10.67	(35)
150mm	4.57	(15)	5.8	(19)	6.86	(22½)	8.23	(27)	10.67	(35)	13.72	(45)	16.15	(53)
180mm	5.49	(18)	7.01	(23)	8.23	(27)	9.75	(32)	12.8	(42)	16.15	(53)	19.51	(64)
250mm	7.63	(25)	9.75	(32)	11.28	(37)	13.72	(45)	17.98	(59)	22.86	(75)	26.82	(88)

Kodak stack loader

Leitz Pradovit

Duplicating

Duplicated transparencies can be as good as or even better than, the originals. Commercial laboratories duplicate transparencies and they can also be made at home using a bellows attachment or electronic machine. Many photographers make dupes of pictures so those can be sent out rather than risking the loss of irreplaceable originals. But duping can also be a creative process, producing images which depend as much on the duping machine as on the camera.

Duplicating is often thought of as a rescue operation. It can be used to save transparencies that are up to one and a half stops underexposed.

Start by duping correctly exposed transparencies with normal filtration and normal development. Having established a norm, experiment with exposure times and filtration.

Kodak make an excellent duplicating film which is available in 30.5m (100ft) rolls to be loaded into cassettes. Ektachrome 64 or 50 (tungsten film) is effective if overexposed one stop with the processing *cut* to correspond. The greatest difficulty when duplicating transparencies is the build-up of contrast—this can be reduced by underdevelopment. If more contrast is desired use Kodachrome 25.

The creative potential of duping is endless. Try double exposing two transparencies onto one picture. Dreamlike effects can be achieved with figures and skyscapes. Images can be enlarged, and it

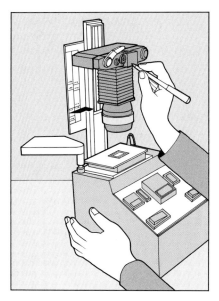

If the camera pentaprism can be removed, images can be outlined on the ground glass, *above*. When making a composite picture, *left*, the originals must be matched—the slightest misplacement will ruin the result.

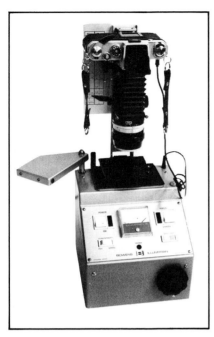

Slide copying attachments, *above*, which fit onto the end of the bellows, are made by most system manufacturers.

With an electronic duplicating machine, *above*, transparencies can be copied easily and quickly. The built-in electronic flash is synced with the camera shutter. Several types of duping machines have a pre-fogging attachment. This overcomes the problem of increased contrast in the duplicated picture.

Slides can be duplicated by shooting with a macro lens. Attach the slide to a sheet of glass and light it from behind with compact flash, covered by a sheet of tracing paper. The flash will illuminate the transparency to be copied. This process demands light of constant quality—daylight varies too much.

is even possible to enlarge one image and leave the other the same size.

Most top-range manufacturers make a camera body with a removable penta-prism. The image to be duplicated can then be traced onto the ground glass viewing screen for reference—useful when making composite pictures which must be matched. With other SLR cameras, use a grid focusing screen to help calculate the position of the image. Alternatively, project the images onto a screen; draw off their outlines and compose the shot to fit.

When exposing two images the exposure time for each must be halved or the result will be overexposed. Using that principle, each exposure can be altered to give the desired emphasis. Although any number of images can be duped together,

keep them simple; multiple images can become confusing.

Once a photographer becomes involved in duplicating slides, images can be shot specifically for superimposition. A stock of sunset pictures, for example, can be put to good use. Fascinating effects can be achieved by duping colour negatives and slides together, or duping onto infrared colour film.

Transparencies with interesting content but unattractive colour may make better black and whites. If so, shoot black and white negatives off the transparencies. Give plenty of exposure and develop in fine grain developer.

If filters are used in a duplicating process place them between the light source and the transparency, not on the lens, which can cause loss of sharpness.

Copying

Bowen's copy stand. The camera screws onto an extension arm which brings it directly over the centre of the artwork. It can also be moved up and down the column. Even lighting is ensured by the four adjustable lights. The complete unit can be made secure by screwing the bracket at the top of the column to a wall. This eliminates camera shake on long exposures.

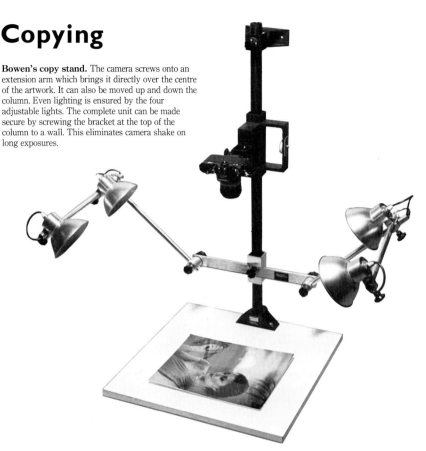

Photographing flat artwork, such as paintings or photographs, is a precise task which requires care and concentration. It is a good technique to master since it can be used so often—for titles and captions to slide shows; for making copies of old family portraits, or photographs for which negatives have been lost; and even for making reproductions of oil paintings or drawings.

Use a spirit level to ensure that the flat artwork and the camera are perfectly square, then mount the camera directly over the centre of the original.

Position lights on each side of the camera, at the same height and at 45° to the painting. If the lights are too close to the artwork they will create reflections off the surface. They must be balanced to give exactly the same exposure from each side. A good method of checking the

position of the lights when setting up is to place a matchbox or pencil in the middle of the artwork and move the lights until the shadow is exactly the same on each side. To be sure of achieving correct exposure take the reading off a grey card.

Reproducing the colour balance of the original is critical. Shots taken on colour negative film can be corrected at print stage. Place a colour scale and a grey scale, obtainable at photographic shops, at one side of the artwork. The printer can then match these scales to his own to achieve correct balance. Colour and grey scales can also be used with transparency film to achieve the correct balance on the reshoot.

If the object being copied has a reflective surface, hold a large piece of black card or cloth around the front of the camera, making a hide for the lens, or use a polarizing filter. If there are still reflections, place sheets of polarizing material over the lights.

Many families have albums or collections of old pictures which have been passed down over generations. Even if they have greatly deteriorated it is not difficult to restore old photographs with a copy set-up.

Use a yellow filter with black and white film to make yellowish stains disappear. Faded images can often be revived with yellow (which increases contrast by lightening light areas and darkening the darks) or a blue filter, which also increases contrast. The yellow filter works better on sepia-toned pictures and the blue on more black and white pictures. Faded edges can be corrected in the darkroom by giving them more exposure than the rest of the print.

Retouch holes and spots on the copy print. If the original sepia quality is to be reproduced, tone the finished print with a sepia kit. Do any retouching in brown tones rather than greys.

Use slow film such as Agfa 25, which is high in contrast and grain-free when processed normally. If a softer result is required overexpose one stop and underdevelop.

If making transparencies for projection from black and white prints use Kodachrome 25 in daylight or electronic flash. Its blue-black tones enhance the image being copied and make very pleasing transparencies. The film is virtually grain free so the grain of the black and white prints looks "punchy" when viewed on a screen.

Artwork can be copied straight off a wall, as long as the camera is parallel with it. Use a pencil or matchbox, *right*, to judge the light level. Make sure the density of shadow is the same both sides.

Mounts and frames

A mounted transparency is easier to handle than a loose piece of film and can be stamped with identifying marks. Process paid film is returned to the customer cut and mounted. Kodachrome comes in cardboard mounts; Agfa and many commercial labs use plastic. Film processed by a commercial laboratory usually comes back unmounted but can be mounted at extra cost.

Professionals who shoot many rolls of film on an assignment cut the best frames from a strip and mount them; many makes of mount are available.

Always use the mounts the same way round with the emulsion side on the same side of the mount. The emulsion side of Ektachrome film is the less shiny side. Kodachrome emulsion is matt with a minute bas-relief appearance.

Frames

A huge variety of picture frames is now readily available, ranging from simple perspex to decorative antique examples. Most are suitable for photographs, but it is essential to marry the right picture to the right frame.

Small, stand-up frames have always been popular for family photographs, but

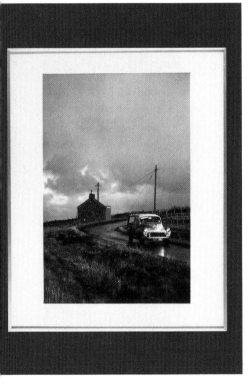

Photographs do not need ornate frames—the simple aluminium style, *above*, is readily available and suits most images. Stores offering a selection of do-it-yourself frames, mounting boards and a quick framing service have proliferated in the last few years and are now a feature of most shopping centres.

Glass protects photographs against dirt and atmospheric conditions. Use a window mount to hold the glass off the print and prevent Newton's rings—annoying bubble images which may appear if the two touch. Cut the inside edges of the mount at an angle of 45°—the white border helps set off the framed picture.

try enlarging your favourite pictures and putting them up on the wall. Select the best from your holiday photographs and display those too; an ordinary small print often comes to life when enlarged.

Such pictures do not need complex framing—a simple aluminium frame compliments most images. Always use mounts. Framing shops supply the board and will cut mounts to size for you. And don't feel that once a picture is framed it has to stay there for ever. Get prints to the same size and ring the changes.

Framed pictures often look more effective when grouped on the wall. Don't just hang them square but arrange them in pleasing shapes; try your arrangement out on the floor until you get it right. Make sure the lighting is good. Don't hang glass-fronted pictures opposite a window unless non-reflective glass is fitted to the frame.

As well as framing individual prints try grouping small prints in a frame. Cut a window in a mount for each picture or simply use a collection of n-prints like a collage. A selection of pictures of a wonderful holiday or even from different stages of someone's life can make the most wonderful gift.

Group a collection of small prints together in a frame to make a memento of a special occasion or tell a story. These pictures show three brothers at various stages of their lives from babyhood to maturity. Cut individual windows in a mount as shown here or simply butt the pictures up to one another to make a simple collage.

Presentation

The potential of photography is only fully realized when finished pictures are presented for others to see—in an album, on a wall as a print, or projected. There is no point in taking great pictures which are then stored out of sight or hung haphazardly. Make a conscious effort and think of this as the show business aspect of photography.

A slide show

Before planning a slide show, album or exhibition, edit the photographs carefully. Selecting pictures requires a different attitude to that needed when taking the photographs. Do not think about how difficult it was to get the pictures or how pleasant the holiday was. Forget the emotional attachment to the pictures and try to select them on their merits.

There is a great difference between choosing one picture to do a specific job and selecting a set to be shown together. Much of the dramatic impact of a selection of shots depends on the juxtaposition of one picture with another. The effect of two sympathetic images added together can be greater than the sum of the two separate pictures. Deliberately jarring images can be placed together to jolt or unsettle the viewer. Experiment with the choice of images to create displays representative of personal taste.

Link the photographs together with a theme. If a shot does not fit in with the central idea it does not belong and must be rejected—no matter how beautiful it is. Rejected pictures will probably come in useful in another context.

The same disciplines apply whether the photographs are intended to create a mood of anger, joy, nostalgia, eroticism or fantasy; or just tell a simple story about a holiday, wedding or sales conference.

Making a portfolio

Professionals carry their best pictures in portfolios to show potential clients examples of their work.

The portfolio will usually contain laminated copies of book and magazine pages showing published photographs, and prints and transparencies mounted on cards.

Laminations are made commercially by sandwiching a print between two pieces of clear plastic and applying heat. The lamination protects the print from

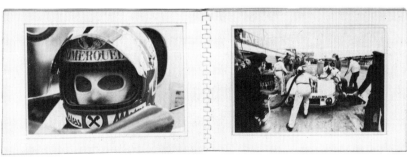

damage and also brightens the colour under a gloss finish. It is a good method to use when a print is likely to be handled frequently.

Transparency cards are black sheets of card with holes cut to accept slide mounts. Protective plastic sheeting covers the top. The cards can be bought or easily made for yourself.

Keeping a portfolio of current photographs is a helpful way to trace improvements in technique. It gives an end product to all the effort as well as keeping the best work readily available. To make a portfolio look its best bear the following points in mind.

In the folder place all the images the same way around.

Keep the portfolio simple. Don't try and include too much to look at.

Include samples of any work which has been published, samples that are relevant to that client, and photographs that are just your own personal favourites and characteristic of your work.

Mount everything cleanly, with one image per page. If images are related, as in a sequence set, for example, they could be mounted together.

A presentation pack should not be so big that it is difficult to find enough desk space to lay it on.

Keep the viewing of transparencies simple. If art directors can get an overall view of transparencies, they can then pick out those that interest them for closer study. Alternatively, mount them singly so they can be looked at individually.

A variety of portfolio cases is available, from soft plastic types to the more expensive model shown here. While it is worth buying the best that can be afforded, make sure it is a manageable size. Don't buy one that is too big to carry or that will take up a great deal of desk space. Insert prints so they can be viewed from one angle, without having to turn the case around.

Spiral bound prints, *left*, can look impressive. Transparencies should be mounted in cards.

Slide show

The family holiday provides a great opportunity to take a mass of pictures. On your return home make a slide show to tell the whole story—the funny moments, the excitement, the great meals and the atmospheric details. Keep the end product in mind when shooting. Back up the key images with sequence shots of less spectacular but interesting events.

Record local music to play as a background track and even try making your own tape of sounds in cafés and city streets, of the laughter of children on the beach, the sound of waves or animal noises. Use any sounds that add atmosphere.

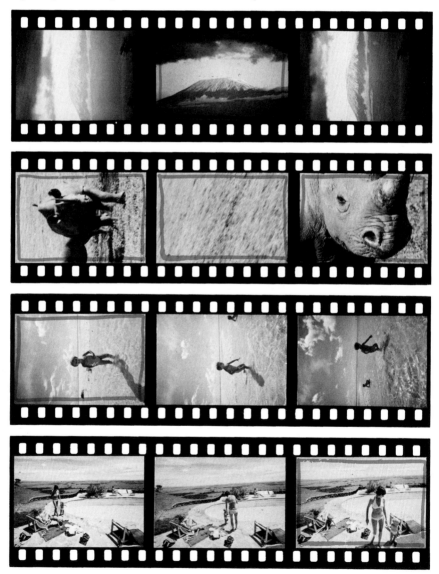

Edit the transparencies on the light box as soon as they are processed. Get all the pictures into chronological order and select the key shots. Then choose link pictures which tie the whole story together. If you have vertical and horizontal versions of the same subject, select one of each to see which is more effective —it can be interesting to use both together. Running several different shots of the same subject can give a more complex impression and add to the pace of the show. If the slide projector is being manually operated it can be speeded up to bring such a sequence of pictures even more to life.

1

2

3

A shot of a passport stamp or map (1) can be used as a title to identify the location. The "Snows of Kilimanjaro" at sunrise (2). This is one of East Africa's greatest landmarks. The Garrett family at the pool of the Mara Serena Lodge (3) overlooking the plains of the Masai Mara.

4

5

6

A rhino about to charge our safari wagon (4). In a moment of terror the photographer loses the rhino from the camera viewfinder (5). Having pulled himself together, the photographer takes a shot of the snorting animal as it approaches the wagon (6).

7

8

9

A detail from a memorable fish lunch on Robinson Island after a long, hard journey (7). Our son Nicholas enjoying the pleasures of the ocean outside the holiday house in Malindi (8). My wife Michelle and self snapped by a friend enjoying a drink in our favourite bar (9).

Applications

Most of the billions of photographs taken every year are shot on vacation. Processing houses report that their best business is done in the summer months and just after Christmas. But it is a pity that so much equipment, and enthusiasm, is not applied during the rest of the year. Photography can add so much to the enjoyment of other hobbies; it can be helpful in a business or merely used to record a full and happy life.

The technical expertise necessary to make daily photography satisfying is easily mastered—with practice and this book. The taking of fine photographs is far more dependent on an interest in what is being photographed. People absorbed in their hobbies, their jobs, their children, using cameras solely to record information and results, can acquire unique collections of pictures. Their *primary* interests are the crucial factor.

But you don't have to be an expert on a subject to take a great photograph relating to it. The camera can be the catalyst between you and your subject and enthusiasm is often more important than knowledge.

If in doubt about what to photograph first ask yourself: "What am I interested in? What excites me? What is beautiful to me? What makes me angry? What makes me laugh?" The answers to such questions can provide enough material to last a lifetime. If the camera records your interests, good pictures will follow.

Almost every hobby or business has its own specialist magazines, which usually welcome pictures that may be of interest to fellow enthusiasts. Send pictures in. If the magazine uses them they may want to see more. No editor or picture editor will ignore good relevant photographs. The publication may only be a small trade paper with a limited budget, but getting pictures published is always a thrill.

Many large companies publish house magazines, which depend on contributions from employees. These can provide a good outlet for the keen photographer who takes news or reportage shots. More

ELM TREE COTTAGE

personal pictures, with artistic or humorous qualities, may also be welcomed by editors of house journals who often have trouble filling their pages.

People who have to travel during the course of their business can find a camera an invaluable notebook, especially if used in conjunction with a pocket cassette recorder.

The number of professions, trades or interests to which photography can be applied is endless. People in creative areas, such as architects or designers, should be well aware of the potential of the camera, but executives, too, could take photographs to embellish company reports. Use the camera as a communications tool.

Estate agents often rely on inadequate snapshots of property to interest buyers. A good photograph of a building will attract more attention from customers than a poor, unsharp snapshot. Those who manage large estates often have to make aerial surveys of the land. Such trips can be recorded with the aid of a camera.

Teachers and lecturers can add interest to their classes with relevant photographs, possibly made up into slide shows.

At the risk of putting professional photographers out of work, it should be pointed out that many of their smaller commissions for lectures, sales conferences, internal house magazine articles, reference or promotion can often be shot satisfactorily by an employee.

Experiences

I was sitting in a café in the Grand Bazaar in Istanbul completely fascinated by an old lady who was sitting silently by her husband as he downed four bottles of beer. Her face was a study of tragic resignation which I found very moving. She was to me a classic symbol of the unliberated woman of that part of the world. Since there was little light, I put the 180mm f2.8 lens on my camera and sat it on top of the soft bag pointing, almost accidentally, toward them, while trying to appear to be taking no interest. Eventually, I composed and took two shots. By the time I took the second, the lady had noticed me, and that was less effective.

Real life shots sometimes require almost infinite patience, but they can say so much more than glossy, superficial pictures.

Time-Life

Die Stern

One Sunday, I was taking a walk with my eighteen-month-old son Nicholas and carrying a Nikkormat EL fitted with an 80–200mm zoom lens and loaded with HP5 film.

We had stopped while Nicholas played with some other children. At one point I turned round to see if Nicholas was alright only to see a bigger boy holding a toy gun to his head. I took a picture of the scene almost instinctively. The camera was on automatic, so I simply had to focus and shoot before the children had a chance to change position.

The picture that resulted was first published in the book *The Family of Children*. It has since been used by the German magazine *Die Stern*; the Italian *Oggi*; the French *Parents*, and the American magazine *Look* to illustrate a variety of articles.

The obvious moral of the story is to carry your camera at all times and become so familiar with your equipment that you can shoot automatically in any situation that arises.

228

The *Observer Magazine* commissioned me to make a picture story of the yearling horse trials in Dublin. The sale yards and stables were new and sterile—no romance there at all. The main interest of the story was in the characters involved in the sales—the Arab princes, *top left*, versus the rest of the world—and they provided some useful pictures for the article.

But by the third day I was concerned that I still had no strong lead picture for the article. I hung on an extra day, hoping for a dramatic photograph with that something extra. This nervous yearling cooperated with me, if not for his handlers.

Often time and a "never give up" attitude can be more important than photographic technique.

Observer Magazine

Sunday Express
Magazine

I was assigned by the *Sunday Express Magazine* to spend a week photographing the life of the Manchester United soccer team. This was during a time when the great club was at a very low ebb. They had been losing consistently, they had a new manager and many of their star players were injured.

I arrived for a Saturday match—they lost. On Wednesday they played a Third Division team in the Cup (a knock-out tournament)—they lost again! The following Saturday was make or break. I

set up a camera with a 600mm lens mounted on a tripod and framed on the manager's dugout—I knew that if they scored the reactions would make a strong picture.

After 70 minutes United did score and I shot this picture even before I got my eye to the viewfinder. I took five shots but this is the first and best.

Anticipation is crucial in reportage photography. I had virtually taken this picture in my mind 70 minutes earlier—all that remained was to push the button.

229

Experiences

In July 1986 I was one of a team of photographers assigned to cover Prince Andrew's wedding for the world's press. A week beforehand, when the press stand was erected, I was allocated a position outside Westminster Abbey and padlocked a set of steps in position to stake my claim.

On the day itself we were there by 6.30 although the wedding did not begin until 11. I took with me four lenses—a 35mm, a 180mm, an 800mm mounted on a tripod and a 300mm on a monopod—and five bodies loaded with film.

When at last the royal couple emerged from the Abbey I shot a roll of film on the 800mm lens in five bursts then changed to the 300mm as they got into the carriage. I then went back to the 800mm for some more intimate shots of Andrew and Sarah in the carriage and continued alternating between the two lenses as they drove away. In the four minutes between the couple coming out of the church and leaving in the carriage I shot three rolls of film. The cover picture was on the third roll.

These occasions are tremendously exciting and you need to keep a cool head to operate successfully under such pressure. One young photographer near me got completely carried away by the thrill of the moment—he shot the whole thing without a film in the camera.

Allied Lyons brochure

Allied Lyons, a leading food and drink company, sent me around the world to photograph different aspects of their work for their corporate brochure. It was a demanding assignment. I had only a short time, often only a day, in each place in which to produce a good picture.

One location was a Harvey's sherry *bodega* in Jerez de la Frontera in Spain. As I walked around deciding what to photograph I noticed that the layout of the cellar was such that in the middle of the day the sun would shine straight through the cellar doors, side-lighting the barrels.

I then found someone to demonstrate the age-old pouring skills used when sampling sherry and positioned him in a pool of light against the background of the barrels. One door was half-closed to mask some light off the barrels so they appeared darker than the man's suit. A small flash lit his shadow areas and enabled me to half-freeze the pouring action.

The resulting picture shows an expert at work, absorbed in his daily activity—something I enjoy photographing and believe always makes a good image.

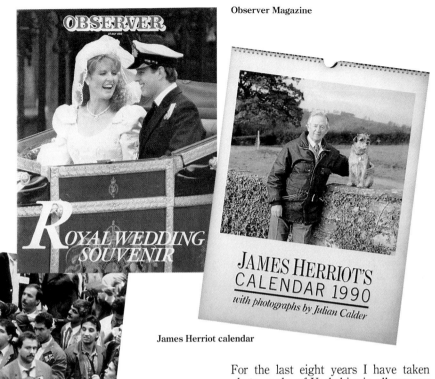

Observer Magazine

Observer Magazine

James Herriot calendar

Business

On assignment for *Business* magazine I visited the Chicago Mercantile Exchange. Like all trading floors it was an impressive sight, with hundreds of people jostling and shouting.

I chose a spot on the balcony looking down on the animated scene. Using a 300mm f2.8 lens with a 30 Magenta filter to correct the fluorescent light, I framed the mass of faces and shot at 1/8 second to keep some movement in the picture.

The picture ran as a double page spread in the magazine—always a gratifying reward for a photographer's efforts.

For the last eight years I have taken photographs of Yorkshire in all seasons and all weathers for the author James Herriot's calendar. I spend about three weeks a year taking the pictures, spread over five or so visits, and have come to know and love this immensely varied area well. There are dramatic landscapes, abbeys and castles, wild coastlines and wonderful characters, a rewarding location for a long-term commission. Weather can be a problem. People seem to prefer sunny pictures for a calendar, but one year I spent 22 days on location before getting a dry day.

When taking pictures for a calendar I have to remember that they will be on the wall for a month, not just looked at briefly before turning the page. I am not taking pictures for myself but to do a certain job and to fit perceptions of Yorkshire.

The calendar may not be great art but I have had a lot of pleasure doing it and hope it gives as much to others.

Recommended books

Photographers are often described as having a "great eye". This is simply the ability to see and isolate great pictures—whether by capturing magical action moments or juxtaposing objects against a studio background. The top photographers have the uncommon in common—a personal vision.

It is an enormous help to study the work of leading photographers when educating the eye. Do not just sit back and applaud them, however. Try to understand why a particular shot was taken, where the light was coming from, the lens and type of film used. Question every aspect of the picture and study the composition.

This list of books is not definitive, but includes those that we have found most stimulating and helpful. They are not all collections of photographs—Norman Rockwell's *America*, for instance, is of interest for the lighting effect in his illustrations. Build up a library slowly and get to know the books by reading and studying them—there is plenty to be learned.

GENERAL
Adams, Ansel *Images* 1923–1974
  (USA) New York Graphic Society
Angel, Heather *The Book of Close-up Photography*
  (UK) Ebury Press
  (USA) Alfred A. Knopf Inc
Brandt, Bill *Shadow of Light*
  (UK) Gordon Fraser
  (USA) Da Capo Press
Eisenstaedt, Alfred *Eisenstaedt's Album*
  (UK) Thames & Hudson
  (USA) Viking Penguin
Feininger, Andreas *The Complete Colour Photographer*
  (UK) Thames & Hudson
  (USA) Prentice-Hall
Fusco, Paul, and McBride, Will *The Photo Essay: How to Communicate with Pictures*
  (UK) Thames & Hudson
  (USA) Alskog
Gerster, Georg *The Grand Design, Flights of Discovery*
  (UK) Paddington Press
  (USA) Paddington Press
Haas, Ernst *In America*
  (UK) Thames & Hudson
  (USA) Viking Penguin

Kane, Art *The Persuasive Image*
  (UK) Thames & Hudson
  (USA) Alskog
Kertesz, André *Sixty Years of Photography*
  (UK) Thames & Hudson
  (USA) Viking Penguin
Lartigue, Henri *Diary of a Century*
  (UK) Penguin Books
  (USA) Viking Penguin
Michals, Duane *The Photographic Illusion*
  (UK) Thames & Hudson
  (USA) Alskog
Penn, Irving *Moments Preserved*
  (USA) Simon & Schuster
Ricciardi, Mirella *Vanishing Africa*
  (UK) Collins
  (USA) Holt, Rinehart & Winston
Rockwell, Norman *Norman Rockwell's America*
  (USA) Harry N. Abrams
Seton, Marie *Biography of Sergei Eisenstein*
  (USA) Evergreen
Sontag, Susan *On Photography*
  (UK) Penguin Books
  (USA) Farrar, Straus & Giroux
Taylor, Herb *Underwater with Nikonos and Nikon Systems*
  (USA) Amphoto
Weston, Edward *50 Years*
  (UK) McGraw Hill Books
  (USA) Aperture
A Day in the Life of China
  (UK) Merehurst Press
  (USA) Collins
A Day in the Life of Spain
  (UK) Collins
  (USA) Collins
The Image Bank: Visual Ideas for the Creative Photographer
  (UK) Phaidon Press
  (USA) Amphoto
The Life Library of Photography
  Time-Life Books
The Cities of the World
  Time-Life Books
The Best of Life
  Time-Life Books

PHOTOJOURNALISM/ REPORTAGE
Brassai *The Secret Paris of the 30s*
  (UK) Thames & Hudson
  (USA) Random House
Cartier-Bresson, Henri *The World of Cartier-Bresson*
  (UK) Gordon Fraser
  (USA) Viking Penguin

Erwitt, Elliott *Photographs and Anti-Photographs*
(UK) Thames & Hudson
(USA) Viking Penguin
Evans, Harold *Pictures on a Page*
(UK) William Heinemann
(USA) Holt, Rinehart & Winston
Frank, Robert *The Americans*
(USA) Aperture
Lange, Dorothea *Dorothea Lange*
(USA) Museum of Modern Art
Mark, Mary Ellen, and Leibovitz, Annie *Photojournalism: The Woman's Perspective*
(UK) Thames & Hudson
(USA) Alskog
Great Photographic Essays from Life
(UK) Life Books
(USA) New York Graphic Society
In Our Time: The World as seen by Magnum Photographers
(UK) Andre Deutsch
(USA) American Federation of Arts

PORTRAITS
Avedon, Richard *Avedon Photographs*
(UK) Thames & Hudson
(USA) Farrar, Straus & Giroux
Avedon, Richard *Nothing Personal*
(UK) Penguin Books
(USA) Atheneum
Avedon, Richard *Observations*
(UK) Weidenfeld & Nicolson
Davidson, Bruce *East 100th Street*
(USA) Harvard University Press
Kirkland, Douglas *Light Years*
(UK) Thames & Hudson
(USA) Thames & Hudson Inc.
Kobal, John *Hollywood Glamour Portraits*
(USA) Dover
Leibovitz, Annie *Rolling Stone: The Photographs*
(USA) Simon & Schuster
Mapplethorpe, Robert *Some Women*
(USA) Secker & Warburg
Skrebneski *Beautiful Women*
(USA) New York Graphic Society

WAR
Burrows, Larry *Compassionate Photographer*
(USA) Time-Life Books
Capa, Robert *Images of War*
(UK) Paul Hamlyn
(USA) Grossman
Duncan, David Douglas *War Without Heroes*
(USA) Harper & Row

Nachtwey, James *Deeds of War*
(UK) Thames & Hudson
(USA) Thames & Hudson Inc.

ANIMALS
Beard, Peter H. *The End of the Game*
(UK) Collins
(USA) Viking Penguin
Erwitt, Elliot *Son of Bitch*
(UK) Thames & Hudson
(USA) Grossman
Reifenstahl, Leni *Coral Gardens*
(UK) Collins
(USA) Harper & Row
Van Lawick, Hugo *Savage Paradise—Victims of the Serengeti*
(UK) Collins
(USA) William Morrow

NUDE
Brandt, Bill *Nudes 1945–1980*
(UK) Gordon Fraser
(USA) New York Graphic Society
Hamilton, David *The Best of David Hamilton*
(UK) Collins
(USA) William Morrow
Newton, Helmut *White Women*
(UK) Quartet Books
(USA) Stonehill
Weston, Edward *Nudes*
(UK) Gordon Fraser
(USA) Aperture

SPORT
Leifer, Neil *Sport*
(USA) Abrams
Zimmerman & Kaufmann *Photographing Sports*
(UK) Thames & Hudson
(USA) Alskog

TRAVEL
Reifenstahl, Leni *The Last of the Nuba* and *People of Kau*
(UK) Collins
(USA) Harper & Row
Singh, Raghubir *The Ganges*
(USA) Perennial Press

CHILDREN
Mason, Jerry *The Family of Children*
(UK) Cape
(USA) Ridge Press

Index

Pictures in this book were either commissioned by or subsequently used by the following:

Ali Razza Corporation
Allied Lyons
Art + Craft Editions Limited
Business
Cosmopolitan
Daily Mirror
Davidson Pearce Berry & Spottiswood
GEO
Independent Broadcasting Authority
  (London)
The Illustrated London News
Look

Malcolm Lauder (ARCA)
Nova
Observer
Oggi
Parents
Paris Match
Playboy
St Martin's Press/Michael Joseph
Scottish Universal Investments
Smithsonian Magazine
Sports Illustrated
Stern
Sunday Telegraph Magazine
The Times
Time-Life Books
Time Magazine

The publishers and authors would like to thank the following for their assistance in the preparation of this book:

Harry Collins, Suzi Keane, John Pitchforth
  and Barry Edmonds of Nikon UK
John Pilger
Richard H. Growald
Dr George Hadfield
Graham Wainwright and David Halliday
  of Leeds Camera Centre, London, for
  providing equipment, advice and
  information
Downtown Darkroom and Robin Bell for
  black and white printing
Sendeans for information on camera
  maintenance
Fred and Kathie Gill for proof reading

Tony Bown, Jacqui Morris and Andy
  Green for photographic assistance
Michelle Garrett for picture selection
Graeme Harris for photographic advice
Jenny Allsopp, Lavinia Scott-Elliot and
  Alison Tomlinson for research and
  general assistance
Judith Beadle for the index

Models: Rosemary Clarke, Una Crawford,
  Kim Greist (Models One), Jane Howard,
  Nancy Howard, Nikki Howath (Petal),
  Soraya (Top Models), Madeline Vale
  (Askew)

Make-up: Julia Hunt

Hair stylist: Barbara Sylvester, Fenwick

Artwork credits

10 Arka; 12–13 reproduced by kind permission of the Nikon Corporation; 15 John Hutchinson; 32 John Hutchinson; 35 John Hutchinson; **39** Arka, John Hutchinson; **46** Arka; **58** Arka, Trevor Hill; 64 John Hutchinson; **65** Arka, Trevor Hill; 66 Trevor Hill, Jim Robins; **68** Trevor Hill, Jim Robins; **70–71** Arka; **72–73** Arka; 74–75 Arka; 77 John Hutchinson; **78–79** Arka, Trevor Hill; **80–81** Arka, Trevor Hill; **82–83** Arka, Trevor Hill; 84–85 John Hutchinson; 86–87 John Hutchinson; **89** Arka, Trevor Hill, John Hutchinson; 90 Arka, John Hutchinson; **92–93** Arka, Trevor Hill; **126–27** Arka; 132 Arka; 133 John Hutchinson; 150 Arka; 154 Trevor Hill, Jim Robins; 163 Jim Robins; **200–1** Arka, Trevor Hill; **202–3** Arka, Trevor Hill; 207 John Hutchinson; 210 Arka; **216** Arka, John Hutchinson; **217** Arka; 219 John Hutchinson

Bold page numbers: artwork from original photographs © Julian Calder

Main photograph credits

Garrett
48, 49 (top left), 50, 51, 52 (centre), 53 (top left, centre), 55 (top, bottom), 56, 57 (left), 63, 69, 94, 95, 98–9, 102–3, 104, 106–7, 110–11, 122, 123 (top left), 130–31, 132–33, 138, 140–41, 144–45, 146, 148–49, 151, 152–53, 155, 156, 157, 160, 161 (bottom), 162 (right), 163 (bottom), 168–69 (3, 5, 7, 8, 11, 13), 171, 185 (top left, bottom right), 193 (bottom right, 195, 224–25, 226, 227 (far left, far right), 228–29

Calder
28–29, 30–31, 32–33, 34–35, 36–37, 41, 42, 45, 49 (centre, bottom right), 50 (bottom left), 51 (bottom left), 52 (top, bottom), 53 (top right, bottom left), 55 (centre), 57 (top right, bottom right), 60–61, 62, 63, 64, 96–97, 100, 101, 105, 108–9, 112–13, 114–15, 116–17, 118–19, 120, 121, 123 (centre, top right, bottom), 124–25, 127, 128, 129, 134–35, 136–37, 139, 142, 143, 158–59, 161 (top), 162 (left), 163 (top), 164–65, 166, 167, 168–69 (1, 2, 4, 6, 9, 10, 12), 170, 172–83, 184, 185 (top right, bottom left), 188, 189, 190, 191, 192, 193 (top, bottom left), 194, 227 (centre top, centre bottom), 230–31